Africa's Liberation

The Legacy of Nyerere

Through the voices of the peoples of Africa and the global South, Pambazuka Press and Pambazuka News disseminate analysis and debate on the struggle for freedom and justice.

Pambazuka Press – www.pambazukapress.org

 A Pan-African publisher of progressive books and DVDs on Africa and the global South that aim to stimulate discussion, analysis and engagement. Our publications address issues of human rights, social justice, advocacy, the politics of aid, development and international finance, women's rights, emerging powers and activism. They are primarily written by well-known African academics and activists. All books are available as ebooks.

Pambazuka News – www.pambazuka.org

 The award-winning and influential electronic weekly newsletter providing a platform for progressive Pan-African perspectives on politics, development and global affairs. With more than 1,500 contributors across the continent and a readership of more than 500,000, Pambazuka News has become the indispensable source of authentic voices of Africa's social analysts and activists.

Pambazuka Press and Pambazuka News are published by Fahamu (www.fahamu.org)

Africa's Liberation

The Legacy of Nyerere

Edited by Chambi Chachage
and Annar Cassam

Pambazuka Press
An imprint of Fahamu Books

Fountain Publishers
Kampala - Uganda

Published 2010 by Pambazuka Press, an imprint of Fahamu Books
Cape Town, Dakar, Nairobi and Oxford
www.pambazukapress.org   www.fahamubooks.org   www.pambazuka.org

Fahamu, 2nd floor, 51 Cornmarket Street, Oxford OX1 3HA, UK
Fahamu Kenya, PO Box 47158, 00100 GPO, Nairobi, Kenya
Fahamu Senegal, 9 Cité Sonatel 2, POB 25021, Dakar-Fann, Dakar, Senegal
Fahamu South Africa, c/o 27A Esher St, Claremont, 7708,
Cape Town, South Africa

Published in Uganda in 2010 by Fountain Publishers Ltd
55 Nkrumah Road, PO Box 488, Kampala, Uganda

First published 2010

British Library Cataloguing in Publication Data
A catalogue record for this book is available from the British Library

UK ISBN: 978-1-906387-71-6 paperback
UK ISBN: 978-1-906387-72-3 ebook
Uganda ISBN: 978-9970-25-000-4

Manufactured on demand by Lightning Source

Contents

About the contributors

Emeka Anyaoku is a former secretary general of the Commonwealth Secretariat 1990–2000.

Ana Camacho is a senior journalist with *El País*, Madrid.

Horace Campbell is professor of political science and African-American studies at Syracuse University, New York.

Annar Cassam is a former personal assistant of President Julius Nyerere.

Chambi Chachage is an independent researcher, newspaper columnist and policy analyst based in Dar es Salaam, Tanzania.

The late **Seithy Chachage** was a professor of sociology at the University of Dar es Salaam.

Ng'wanza Kamata is a political science lecturer at the University of Dar es Salaam and the chair of the Land Rights Research and Resources Institute (LARRRI/HAKIARDHI) board.

Faustin Kamuzora is an associate professor of economic development and development informatics at Mzumbe University, Tanzania.

Helen Kijo-Bisimba is the executive director of the Legal and Human Rights Centre (LHRC), Tanzania.

Firoze Manji is the executive director of Fahamu – Networks for Social Justice and the editor-in-chief of Pambazuka News.

Salma Maoulidi is the executive director of the Sahiba Sisters Foundation in Dar es Salaam, Tanzania.

Marjorie Mbilinyi is a former professor of development studies at the University of Dar es Salaam, based at the Tanzania Gender Networking Programme (TGNP).

Neema Ndunguru is an independent project consultant and writer based in Dar es Salaam.

The late **Haroub Othman** was professor of development studies at the University of Dar es Salaam.

Chris Maina Peter is a professor of law at the University of Dar es Salaam.

Nawal El Saadawi is an Egyptian writer, activist and doctor of medicine whose many books have been translated into over 30 languages.

Mohamed Sahnoun is a former assistant secretary general of the Organisation of African Unity (OAU, 1964–74).

Issa G. Shivji is the Mwalimu Nyerere Professor of Pan-African Studies at the University of Dar es Salaam.

Vicensia Shule is a performing artist and an assistant lecturer at the Department of Fine and Performing Arts, University of Dar es Salaam.

Preface

How we wish you were here: a tribute to Mwalimu Nyerere

Firoze Manji

Ten years ago, on 14 October 1999, a giant died and left a cavern in our consciousness, if not in our conscience: Julius Kambarage Nyerere, the first president of Tanzania, known to us all as 'Mwalimu', a name that, as Nawal El Saadawi points out (see page 7), immediately brings to mind the other giants of the liberation movement – Nkrumah, Lumumba, Nehru, Tito, Nasser, Cabral and many others.

Mwalimu's influence went well beyond the territory that he led to independence. Perhaps a tragedy of all great people is that they are truly recognised for their achievements only after their passing. As Tanzanian people reel under the impact of the concessions subsequent governments have made to the international finance institutions, as they suffer the assault of neoliberal policies, it is really only now that many have begun to realise the extraordinary achievements of the Nyerere years. Whatever criticism many of us may have had during his lifetime – and continue to have – about some of his policies, there is no getting away from the transformations that he brought about. One has only to look at the scale of theft and pillaging, the failure of the national project, the politicisation of ethnic identity, the open collusion with transnational corporations in the plunder of resources that characterise neighbouring countries to understand what efforts Mwalimu made to prevent the same happening in Tanzania. One only has to look at the speed with which Tanzania has played catch-up once

Mwalimu ended his term as president in 1985, to be reminded how different things were.

'Kambarage Nyerere,' sings Neema Ndunguru in this book (see page 1):

> How we wish you were here.
> ... But dear Mwalimu, why didn't you tell us, expose and prepare us
> For the turmoil and struggles that have now engulfed us?

Nyerere was not simply a player on the national terrain. He was a Pan-Africanist and an internationalist – not only in his thoughts and writings, but crucially in his praxis. The support and refuge he provided to the liberation movements was unprecedented. His commitment to welcoming and integrating refugees into Tanzanian life and citizenship was extraordinary. And his willingness to speak out loud against injustices across the world, including – and especially – about Palestine marks him out from the many so-called leaders who have come to be known more for their betrayal than any commitment to political principles. Consider the outstanding act of solidarity he undertook in the 1970s, seeking to break the isolation of Zambia through the building of the 200-km TAZARA railway – an extraordinary logistical enterprise that was a demonstration of South–South cooperation involving Zambia, Tanzania and China (Monson 2009). There can be few comparable ventures in the history of the continent.

We should not be shy in celebrating his achievements. But at the same time, he would be the first to condemn any attempts to romanticise his period in office. This book, parts of which were originally published as a special issue of Pambazuka News in October 2009, seeks both to celebrate Nyerere and to reflect on some of the shortcomings of his policies. Since he retired as president, a whole generation of young people has grown up, many of whom have had little opportunity to read about Mwalimu, to understand why his memory evokes such emotion, and to forge their own views about his contribution.

Pambazuka Press is therefore proud to be publishing this book on Nyerere's legacy. We are grateful to our guest editors, Chambi Chachage and Annar Cassam, for their efforts in making this happen.

Reference

Monson, J. (2009) *Africa's Freedom Railway: How a Chinese Development Project Changed Lives and Livelihoods in Tanzania,* Bloomington, IN, Indiana University Press

Introduction

Annar Cassam

The words 'living memory' acquire a deeper meaning when one considers the place that Mwalimu Julius Nyerere occupies in the minds, hearts, lives, consciousness and subconscious of those who knew him and those who did not, those who live in Tanzania and those who do not, those who pay attention to Africa and those who judge it, from near or afar.

The collection of tributes contained in this compilation were originally sent in spontaneous answer to an invitation from the editor of Pambazuka News for a special issue to celebrate Mwalimu's life and memory on the tenth anniversary of his death in October 1999. The response showed that, ten years later, the memory of him lives on certainly, but also that his words, actions, achievements and shortcomings have now acquired a sharper focus and relevance to our world. It is as though the passing of time has given us a perspective which enables us not only to judge and measure his life and work but also our own contemporary age and place in this 21st century as it unfolds.

The contemporaneous quality is evident in the tributes from Seithy Chachage ('Reading history backwards'), from Chambi Chachage ('Mwalimu in our popular imagination') and in Neema Ndunguru's poem. These are very personal evocations from members of different generations of what it is that they have absorbed from Mwalimu, as much as about him.

The late Haroub Othman ('An intellectual in power') gives us the perspective of the intellectual and academic that he himself was, describing the way Mwalimu, the thinker, the philosopher, managed power – creatively and generously and above all, purposefully, for the purpose was always the human being. Issa Shivji ('The village in Mwalimu's thought and political practice'), another academic, judges from the viewpoint of those on whose behalf that power was held and promoted, not always successfully perhaps.

Two leading feminist figures, Marjorie Mbilinyi (on 'People-centred leadership') and Salma Maoulidi (on 'Racial and religious tolerance') look at Tanzanian society today and see the gaps and the fault lines that are now visible in the two fundamental areas of national construction to which Mwalimu gave his utmost, namely, democracy and its institutions and the imperatives of tolerance and respect for all, without exception.

For the reader who wishes to understand why Tanzania was, and is, a unique case, the chapters on Mwalimu and land, economic development, culture, education, and human rights by Ng'wanza Kamata, Faustin Kamuzora, Vicensia Shule, Chambi Chachage and Helen Kijo-Bisimba and Chris Maina Peter respectively should help. These are the achievements, recorded and explained, which Tanzanians can claim as their own today as they watch the fires burn in their neighbourhood and realise 'what efforts Mwalimu made to prevent the same happening in Tanzania', as Firoze Manji puts it in his Preface.

Horace Campbell's tribute ('Between state-centred and people-centred Pan-Africanism') covers the historical and the personal, the tangible and the silent impact of Mwalimu's liberating self-confidence on the African diaspora of North America, most emphatically in relation to the liberation of Africa from colonialism and racist minority rule. In 1969, the University of Toronto awarded Mwalimu an honorary doctorate and in his acceptance speech, he spelt out a few principles on the subject of liberation the like of which had not been heard before – and will very likely never be heard again – by his august audience:

Tanzania must support the struggle for liberation ... regardless of the political philosophy of those who are conducting the struggle. If they are capitalists, we must support them, if they are liberals, we must support them, if they are communists, we must support them, if they are socialists, we must support them. We support them as nationalists. The right of a man to stand upright as a human being in his own country comes before questions of the kind of society he will create once he has that right. Freedom is the only thing that matters until it is won.

The totality of his commitment to the freedom of others, regardless of their political affiliations and the universality of his belief in the unity of Africa and of other oppressed people gave Mwalimu considerable strength and confidence. From the very beginning of his career, first as a nationalist for Tanganyika's independence and then as internationalist leader of a Third World country, he led the newly formed international organisations of the day, the Organisation for African Unity (OAU) and the Commonwealth particularly, to find their identity and purpose in action.

This is evident in the first-hand testimony provided by two eminent international civil servants, Chief Emeka Anyaoku from Nigeria and Mohamed Sahnoun from Algeria, who were selected to serve at the Commonwealth and the OAU respectively and who collaborated with Mwalimu in the strategy for liberation from the early 1960s. Chief Anyaoku in his interview ('Nyerere and the Commonwealth') and Mohamed Sahnoun in his memoir ('Nyerere, the Organisation of African Unity and liberation') both share their living memory of Mwalimu and of the inspiration he provided in and for their mission.

We hear Mwalimu's own voice as he speaks to two journalists (Nawal El Saadawi of Egypt in 1984 and Ana Camacho of Spain in 1991). Mwalimu speaks in clear and concentrated form about some of the profound beliefs that guided his own action. For example, in the interview with Nawal El Saadawi (for *El Mussawar*, Cairo), he gives a brief record of his 30 years of leadership, of the independence struggle, of nation-building based on the foundations of equality, democracy and socialism, of the liberation struggle and of African and international solidarity.

Looking back at the historical record of all that has happened since 1984, his achievements in building a peaceful, united and stable Tanzania and the success of his strategies for the liberation struggle in southern Africa speak for themselves. A second reason for choosing these interviews lies in their timing. The year 1984 was the last year of his presidency; he retired as head of state exactly a year later in November 1985, his head held high after having faced down relentless pressure and animosity from the International Monetary Fund, the World Bank and other members of the Washington consensus.

The 1991 interview with Ana Camacho (for *El Pais*, Madrid)

occurred at a major turning point in post-war world history, a moment symbolised by the collapse of the Soviet Union and its empire and by the subsequent jubilation expressed by the West. The imploding of the Soviet system, caused mainly by its own contradictions, was seized upon by the USA and Europe as being a vindication of their own form of capitalism. According to them, it was irrefutable proof for all time of the superiority of the West.

Mwalimu, no longer president and having resigned as chairman of the Chama cha Mapinduzi—CCM (The Revolutionary Party) in 1990, speaks with insight and foresight about the Soviet collapse and the ensuing victory dance by the West. About the USSR, he says it is not possible to build socialism without freedom, and about the so-called free market, he warns against worshipping a 'new god' whose days, too, are numbered.

Finally, these two interviewers (both women) demonstrate in their choice of questions serious background knowledge about Mwalimu's career and beliefs and a real understanding of his place in the history of Africa and the world. And both of them show the relevance of Mwalimu's analyses to the political situations prevailing in their own countries and regions.

My co-editor, Chambi Chachage, and I are deeply indebted to Firoze Manji of Pambazuka News and Pambazuka Press for his offer to compile these tributes in a book. As fellow-East Africans, we cannot express our surprise but we can and do express our gratitude for the vibrant homage he himself has provided in the Preface and for the support and solidarity he has given to two novices in the book publishing business. Our sincere thanks and our admiration go to Shereen Karmali for her professional and technical advice and for her rigorous attention, on our behalf, to timelines and deadlines. To Alex Free, we also express our appreciation and thanks. Needless to say, the co-editors alone are responsible for any errors and inaccuracies that may inadvertently have introduced themselves into the text.

A short biography of Julius Nyerere

Madaraka Nyerere

Julius Nyerere was born on 13 April 1922 in Butiama village on the shores of Lake Victoria, the son of Chief Nyerere Burito of the small Zanaki ethnic group. His mother, Christina, was the fifth of the chief's 22 wives.

Mwalimu Nyerere studied at Mwisinge Primary School in Musoma (walking 26 miles a day from home to school) and at the Catholic Mission Secondary School of St Mary's, Tabora. In 1946 he obtained a diploma in education from Makerere University College in Uganda and returned to Tabora to teach. In 1949, he was the first Tanganyikan student to be sent to Edinburgh University from where he graduated in 1952 with an MA in history and economics.

Upon his return to Tanganyika, he was appointed to teach at St Francis Secondary School, Pugu, outside Dar es Salaam, where he also joined the Tanganyika African Association, an unofficial political organisation which was later to become the Tanganyika African National Union (TANU), the nationalist party. Mwalimu was elected president of TANU in 1954 but was forced by the British authorities to choose between teaching and politics. He chose the latter, entered the Legislative Council in 1958 and became its chief minister in 1960. In May 1961, he became prime minister of the self-governing territory of Tanganyika, which he led to full independence from the British in December 1961. In 1962, the country became a republic and Mwalimu was elected its first president. He remained chairman of TANU until 1977 when the party, still under his leadership, became the Chama cha Mapinduzi or the CCM.

In 1963, together with the heads of state of other independent African states, he adopted the Charter of the Organisation of African Unity in Addis Ababa, and invited the newly formed OAU Liberation Committee to establish its headquarters in Dar es Salaam. In 1964, following the overthrow of the British protected sultanate of Zanzibar, Mwalimu and the new leaders of the island agreed to unite to form the United Republic of Tanzania in April 1964.

Under the auspices of the OAU, Tanzania, under Mwalimu's leadership, provided crucial moral and material support to the liberation movements of Africa and later, after the independence of Mozambique and Angola, to the struggle for freedom in Southern Africa through his chairmanship of the Frontline States.

Throughout his political career and in his personal life, Mwalimu remained committed to the promotion of human dignity, equality and social justice, ideals which were set forth in the Arusha Declaration, the national policy framework which was adopted in 1967. On the international front, his strong advocacy for the rights of the poor earned him the unrelenting hostility of the World Bank, the International Monetary Fund and the so-called Washington consensus.

In 1985, he voluntarily stepped down as president after nearly 30 years of leadership, to be succeeded by Ali Hassan Mwinyi of Zanzibar. He remained head of the political party, the CCM, until 1990.

In 1986, Mwalimu began his 'international career' when he was asked by the summits of the Commonwealth and the Non-Aligned Movement to set up the South Commission for the benefit of developing countries and their objectives in the international arena. He and the independent body he appointed produced the report of the South Commission, called the *Challenge of the South*, in 1990. In 1991, he established the South Centre in Geneva, a unique intergovernmental organisation which fosters cooperation and exchange over global economic and developmental strategies for the countries of the Third World. He was chairman of the South Centre until his death in 1999.

One of his last tasks was to be the UN's chief facilitator for the Burundi peace negotiations between 1994 and 1999.

Mwalimu Nyerere died of leukaemia at St Thomas' Hospital, London, on 14 October 1999 and was buried at his village of Butiama after being accorded a funeral with the highest honours by those who respected him at home and abroad.

Adarsh Nayar

Julius Nyerere 1922-1999

This book is dedicated to
the youth of Africa

But Dear Mwalimu

Neema Ndunguru

Kambarage Nyerere,

How we wish you were here.

Thank you for your patience and for making us persevere.

But dear Mwalimu, why didn't you tell us, expose and prepare us

For the turmoil and struggles that have now engulfed us?

Why didn't we continue to build ourselves, our capacities and our attitudes?

And recognise the potential that is within us?

Appreciate the beauty of our land?

Protect and respect the abundance of our resources?

Why weren't we encouraged and persuaded to think beyond our limitations?

To serve our country and be duly recognised for our efforts?

We remained suffering as we looked in awe at those outside our borders.

As though their grass was greener than those of our majestic hills.

As though their water was fresher than that of our sparkling rivers.

We invited them in.

And they saw that which we never saw in ourselves.

They've come to take it. And here we remain. Still … having peace.

Kambarage Nyerere,

Thank you for the peace you promoted in this country.

A solid foundation of humanity.

We've loved our nation. But we've never embraced ourselves.
So where do we go from here? And how do we change our steps?
Dear Mwalimu Julius Kambarage Nyerere.
Things may have been a little different if you were here.
How we wish you were here.

Mwalimu in our popular imagination: the relevance of Nyerere today

Chambi Chachage

His is still the most popular name in Tanzania today. He nowadays arouses citizenry sentiments on any contemporary issue. A humble man, Mwalimu Julius Kambarage Nyerere would shy away from such glory.

It was just the other day that I was on my way from Dar es Salaam to Arusha when I overheard an interesting conversation. In the bus the driver was discussing current issues of national concern with some passengers.

The name 'Nyerere' came up over and over again. This Mwalimu, one passenger quipped, is responsible for what is happening now in our society. There followed a deafening silence.

Well I thought, here again goes a popular Nyerere-bashing with no defence whatsoever as the passenger went on and on, attempting to show how a man who died 10 years ago set into motion what is happening today. Just as I was thinking that the battle for a balanced view on Nyerere had been lost, another passenger chipped in. What he said affirmed what I think is the main legacy of the Mwalimu in Nyerere: the ability to generate public debate on issues of importance to society.

So suddenly the discussion shifted to the other side of the story, as this other passenger started to narrate another conventional history of how Nyerere fostered unity and tranquillity. Other passengers also supported his narrative by noting how Mwalimu had promoted Kiswahili to that end. Surprisingly, the earlier critic seemed to switch camps as he exclaimed and nodded in agreement,

especially after the driver cited Nyerere's call to let Tanzania's min-
erals remain in the ground until we had educated our engineers to
be able to mine them for our own benefit as a nation.

To those of us who are interested in local popular knowledge,
it was such an intellectually stimulating and socially activating
moment to hear the driver link what Nyerere had said with the
ongoing plunder of our natural resources by multinationals such
as Barrick Gold and AngloGold Ashanti.[1] This shows the extent to
which our popular imagination is becoming highly conscious of
the pitfalls of the neoliberal reform strategy of making us LIMP,
that is, liberalised, marketised and privatised. Those words recited
by the driver, by the way, have many popular versions such as:

'Nyerere once said, "We will leave our mineral wealth in the
ground until we manage to develop our own geologists and mining engineers."'[2]

'They have the law behind them – but should a stone that is
found in Tanzania only be monopolised by a foreign company?
President Nyerere said that this is the property of our children!'[3]

Ironically, this popular quote is invoked by politicians who in
one way or another have been behind the LIMP-ing of the mining
sector. In parliamentary sessions variations on this phrase have
been quoted more than once. Interestingly, even the immediate
former prime minister once paraphrased it when he was addressing mining investors.

You can indeed pick virtually any topical issue – from agriculture to Zimbabwe – and Nyerere the teacher will have something
to do with it. Yes, there are tumultuous historical moments of our
times, such as the post-9/11 'War on terror', that he did not live to
see and comment on. Yet in a prophetic way he addressed matters
which related – and indeed which led – to these moments way
back in 1976 in 'The world: message to America from Tanzania's
President Julius K. Nyerere', as published by *Time*:

> We watch with respect, sympathy and anxiety – and sometimes
> almost with despair – as Americans endeavour to cope with
> the political and moral results of their own wealth-creating
> economic system, and to give international meaning to the
> principles laid down by the founding fathers of their nation...
> Americans have created a power which is frequently abused

internally and externally. But Americans continue to struggle against these abuses and for the survival of the universal principles enunciated in 1776. There is therefore still hope that America's great power will be used for human beings everywhere, rather than simply for the preservation and creation of American national wealth.[4]

What about the ongoing economic crunch one may ask – did he also foresee that? We may have not understood his 'stiff-necked' attitude in the wake of the structural adjustment programmes (SAPs), especially when he said 'No to IMF meddling' in 1980. Wasn't he far ahead of his time – way beyond the era of the crestfallen neoliberal project – when he said the following stinging words while addressing diplomats during the 1980 Arusha conference on 'Restructuring the international monetary system':[5]

When did the IMF become an International Ministry of Finance? When did nations agree to surrender to it their power of decision making?

Your Excellencies: It is this growing power of the IMF and the irresponsible and arrogant way in which it is being wielded against the Poor that has forced me to use my opportunity to make these unusual remarks in a New Year Speech to you. The problem of my country and other Third World countries are grave enough without the political interference of IMF officials. If they cannot help at the very least they should stop meddling.[6]

That was Nyerere at his best, the Mwalimu we are commemorating today as we reflect on the popular themes that preoccupied his lifelong learning. This is how Seithy Chachage captured our pan-African imagination when we mourned his physical departure over 10 years ago:

On 14th October 1999 Mwalimu passed away after battling against chronic leukeamia – the disease which killed Frantz Fanon in 1961. The millions of the oppressed people of Africa and the world mourned his loss with profound sadness and a sense of loss, because he is among those people who in words and deeds worked for the empowerment of the powerless. It is for this reason that his influence has never been comforting for those who would like to see people revolt against the noble human ideals he extolled. SAFM (the [South African] radio station for the well informed!) announced his death first on 28th September and 11th October 1999. In both occasions, it apologised for the wrong information. Tim Modise of the same radio station in his 'famous' show on 18th October 1999 quipped cryptically: 'People will ask why should somebody who died in another country concern us so much? Why not go on with our own business?'

South Africans were indeed concerned because of the role Nyerere played in the fight against apartheid, among other social vices. SABC (South African Broadcasting Corporation) even showed his funeral live. Such is how one of the finest sons of Africa permeated that country's imagination.

In sum, the durability of Nyerere's legacy in generating passionate public debate aimed at bringing positive social and economic change is what 'Mwalimu in our popular imagination' is all about. I think it is thus fitting to close this reflection on him with one of his mottoes appropriated across the socialist–capitalist ideological divide: 'It can be done, play your part'!

Notes

1. K. Sharife (2009) 'Tanzania's pot of gold: not much revenue at the end of the rainbow', *Pambazuka News*, issue 450, http://www.pambazuka.org/en/category/features/59142, accessed 8 December 2009.
2. Comment left on 'Nyerere and IMF: will our leaders deliver in the summit?', (2009) *Politics, Society & Things*, http://taifaletu.blogspot.com/2009/03/nyerere-and-imf-will-our-leaders.html, accessed 8 December 2009.
3. Mererani citizen at a community meeting, quoted in CMI report (2006) 'Benefit streams from mining in Tanzania: case studies from Geita and Mererani', *Chr. Michelsen Institute (CMI)*, http://www.cmi.no/publications/publication/?2398=benefit-streams-from-mining-in-tanzania, accessed 8 December 2009.
4. J.K. Nyerere (1976) 'The world: message to America from Tanzania's President Julius K. Nyerere', *Time*, 26 July http://www.time.com/time/magazine/article/0,9171,914388-1,00.html, accessed 8 December 2009.
5. J.K. Nyerere (1980) 'No to IMF meddling', *Another Development: Approaches and Strategies*, Dag Hammarskjöld Foundation, Uppsala, Sweden, vol. 2, pp.7–9
6. J.K. Nyerere (1980).

President Nyerere talks to
El Mussawar (1984)

Interviewed by Nawal El Saadawi

Nyerere's name brings to my mind the names of the leaders of the 1960s – Nkrumah, Lumumba, Nehru, Tito – leaders who, with Gamal Abdel Nasser, led the two huge continents of Africa and Asia towards unity within the Non-Aligned Movement and the Organisation of African Unity. Those years were full of hope, but then came the 1970s to abort these hopes. Now we are in the 1980s and Africa is being buffeted more and more by crises as heavy as the waves of the sea in a storm. Now the continent which is rich in natural resources suffers from problems of food supply. Nyerere rules his country, Tanzania, like the captain of a ship, steering his vessel to avoid the deep currents and the whirlpools. In doing so, he has made his country an island of stability while still continuing to be an African leader who has never stopped struggling.

When you meet him, he is as calm as the waters of Msasani Bay where he lives in Dar es Salaam, and as delicate as a poet. He also writes poetry. He is as simple as a child when he laughs, and as modest as are the truly great. When you sit with him, you yourself feel great; he never seeks to dominate you but gives you all the space in which to be yourself.

He greatly admired Nasser; they worked together for the liberation of the African continent from colonialism. Many times during the last 20 years he has played a historical role in preventing the division of the Organisation of African Unity (OAU).

Although his country is poor in financial resources, he has consistently refused to accept foreign aid under unacceptable conditions or at the expense of his country's independence. He rejected West German aid for the sake of Zanzibar's independence; he

7

sacrificed British aid for the sake of Rhodesia's independence; he continues to resist Reagan for the sake of Namibian and South African independence. And for the sake of his support for the Palestinians, he sacrifices much. During the October 1973 [Arab–Israeli] war, he spoke up against Israel and closed the Israeli embassy in Dar es Salaam. In 1974, he opened the Palestinian embassy whose flag still flies in the capital.

I sat down beside Julius Nyerere at the hour before sunset on the terrace of his house by the sea, the mango and the papaya trees and tropical flowers around us in profusion. He has lived in his own house in Dar es Salaam for the past 20 years – from soon after independence. Behind me was a blackboard where his children used to write and in the corner was a huge receiver-set through which he can follow debates in Parliament. There were no carpets on the floor; the leather-covered chairs were old. I called him 'Mwalimu Nyerere' as his own people do. He is kind-hearted and has a sense of humour. He laughed frequently while commenting on the contradictions of our world. I forgot I was with a head of state. The hour-and-a-half passed by very swiftly. And so I began with my questions.

El Saadawi: We have followed closely the support you have constantly given to the Arabs. You never stopped supporting Egypt even though you did not like Camp David. You have also always supported the cause of the Palestinians. How do you see their struggle?

Nyerere: We have never hesitated in our support for the right of the people of Palestine to have their own land. Our generation was a generation of nationalists struggling for the independence of our own countries – that is what we were there for – but the plight of the Palestinians is very different and much worse. When we were fighting for our independence, I was *in* Tanganyika, Kenyatta was *in* Kenya. Even now, the Namibians and the South Africans are in their *own* country. But the Palestinian plight is more terrible and unjust; they have been deprived of their own country, they are a nation without a land of their own. They therefore deserve the support of Tanzania and the entire world. The world must hear their voice and give them understanding and support. As for supporting the Arab world, you must remember that I believe very strongly in unity. Sometimes, I am accused of supporting unity for its own sake, but I believe that unity is an instrument of liberation. And the oppressed must not easily give up their unity – only the enemy can rejoice at its loss. One of my major statements on unity was made in Cairo in a speech at Cairo University in 1964. At that time, both Nasser and Nkrumah were getting impatient with the 'reactionaries' in our continent, but I said we should not have a confrontation with other African countries; they were a part of us and we all had to live with each other.

Many years later, when some Arab countries tried to have Egypt expelled from the OAU, I defended the unity of the OAU. We can criticise Egypt, I said, but we can never expel an African state from the OAU – where will it end? Similarly, during the Non-Aligned summit of 1979 in Havana, there was an attempt on the part of some Arab countries to expel Egypt from the Non-Aligned Movement. I was asked to join them but I argued that Egypt was a member of the OAU and as such could not be expelled from the Non-Aligned Movement. We will destroy the OAU, and our unity through it, if we begin expelling each other. Egypt is a vital member of the Arab world and of Africa. Sadat went too far in embracing Israel; he was alone because of this; the Arab countries felt betrayed by him. But Africa too lost Egypt – it made a tremendous difference to us, this absence of Egypt. What is the OAU without Egypt? Egypt was a pillar of the OAU, of the Non-Aligned Movement. Earlier this year, President Mubarak came to visit Tanzania, his visit was a success and I believe he is now playing an important role in the Arab world and in Africa.

El Saadawi: What about your relations with Libya?

Nyerere: We have never cut our relations with Libya; Gaddafi got entangled in the Uganda war against us without really meaning to. Idi Amin was a good actor and pretended Uganda was a Muslim country. Amazingly, many other countries were also taken in by him. Uganda is not a Muslim country; it is a Christian country, almost as Christian as Southern Sudan. I tried to explain all this to Gaddafi in 1973 when I met him for the first time in Algiers during the Non-Aligned summit. He had some very vague ideas then about Tanzania. He thought that during the revolution in Zanzibar [1964], Christians had fought against Muslims. I told him that Zanzibar was 99 per cent Muslim and the Zanzibaris, during their revolution, had got rid of their feudalists just as he had got rid of the feudalists in Tripoli in 1969. I wanted to explain this and so get Gaddafi off that hook. He also felt that Tanzania was a Christian country because I am a Christian, but we are very mixed in Tanzania and we have three times more Muslims here than in Libya. However, we are also very secular and we do not believe that politics and religion go together in that sense. I never wanted to make a big issue out of Libya's involvement in the Uganda war. Since then, I have tried to get our friend Gaddafi to understand and I think he now has a greater appreciation of what is happening in this part of the world.

El Saadawi: There is no doubt that African unity is now facing another crisis, especially with the signing of the Nkomati non-aggression pact between Mozambique and South Africa.[1] What are your views on this?

Nyerere: Up to 1980, the liberation struggle went extremely well and we achieved the independence of Zimbabwe. We were then very optimistic about Namibia's independence, and in a sense, we had South Africa on the defensive. Now the situation has changed. South Africa is on the attack. It is bad enough that she is on the offensive against her own people inside South Africa and Namibia, but she is also on the attack against the Frontline States, with full American support. The Americans are backing South African aggression against us – they approve of this policy. So the destabilisation is succeeding. We do not like what is happening in Mozambique, but the South Africans and the Americans are jubilant. We understand why the Frelimo government was forced to reach some agreement with South Africa, but we can no more rejoice at this than could the Arabs over Camp David. The Americans support South Africa and are now saying how wonderful it is that there is an agreement between South Africa and Mozambique! It is a source of humiliation for us but of jubilation for them – this defines their attitude towards us as human beings.

For Mozambique, thing have got worse since Nkomati, and Angola has learnt its lesson from this – that to let the Cubans leave Angola now would be suicide. So there will be no independence for Namibia because of the American linkage [the Reagan government's link between the departure of Cuban forces from Angola and the settlement of Namibian independence as per UN Resolution 435]. South Africa's interest in Angola is to get rid of the MPLA government and install UNITA instead, an ambition shared by the Americans. So we will continue the struggle and we will continue to avoid the division of the Frontline States. We do not want the American-supported offensive to divide us as Camp David divided the Arabs. We believe in unity and so we will remain together.

El Saadawi: The economic problems facing Africa and the Third World are getting worse. America leads the countries of the North in hindering all progress in the South. How do you feel about this now?

Nyerere: These problems are enormous and I do not feel optimistic. We are not going to see much movement – or even sympathy – from the North about our problems in the next few years. The arguments for change are there and are well known but we will not see any change because the Americans do not want any change. And this suits the other countries of the North. They do not like America's attitude towards their own problems but they are not willing to move ahead without the US and adopt policies for the benefit of the South that the Americans oppose.

This was clear to me at the North–South summit in Cancun [Mexico 1981]. There, some 22 countries of the North and the South met to see whether we could get the main leaders of the industrialised world to appreciate our problems and so do something about them. Prior to Cancun, there had been two meetings, the Commonwealth summit at Melbourne [hosted by Prime Minister Malcolm Fraser] and the meeting of the industrialised seven at Ottawa [hosted by Prime Minister Pierre Trudeau], where some basic ideas had been hammered out. At Cancun, it was clear to me that the major leaders of the North – Canada, France, UK, Japan – fully understood the situation and accepted the need for action on the specific problems of global negotiations and an energy affiliate for the World Bank. There was a general consensus on these points but Reagan, alone, opposed us and that was that. It was then also clear to me that the other members of the North were not prepared to move without the US. The Americans have the veto and therefore we will see no movement.

But I am also pessimistic about the South. Just as the North, so the Third World too is afraid of moving in spite of the fact that we possess so many resources. It is not a question of money either – the Third World has it too. At one time, there was the suggestion of a tri-partite form of cooperation to help the Third World develop through a combination of European technology, Arab money and African raw materials. But we have only ourselves to blame; we lack the will to use our own resources for our own liberation.

El Saadawi: It is clear that your concepts of socialism and democracy are your own, based on the belief that socialism can be realised without class conflict and democracy without a multiparty system. Are your ideas still the same or have they changed after 30 years of practical experience?

Nyerere: My political education was of the western liberal type up to the time of independence and so I believed in the multiparty model. But in the struggle for independence, we organised our independence party extremely well. We then found ourselves in the ridiculous position of behaving as if we had a multiparty system with only one party! So we decided, out of necessity, to legalise the fact that we were a single party. Ironically, it was necessary for us to do this in order to introduce some form of democracy into the country because otherwise, our own TANU party would have continued to win all the seats – no other party ever acquired a single member and we were returned unopposed.

In Parliament too, we behaved as if there was another party in the house but there was no debate there at all because there was no opposition. This was a ridiculous situation so we had to legalise the one-party system and then have opposition inside it in order to have democracy and debate. This has had extremely good results. It has given this country one of its major strengths – unity. Of course unity is based on many different things but the unity we have built through the one-party system has been a very strong one because it has also allowed the party to articulate the reasonable aspirations of the majority of our people. Philosophically speaking, I am not a believer in the one-party system exclusively; my own inclination is towards a multiparty system but I do not regard that system to be the only way to democracy. We have tremendous debate and opposition in our party. We are a mass party, not a vanguard party, and we have the whole spectrum of opinions in our party of two million members. This fact has also helped us to contribute to the struggle for liberation – our mass party gave us the unity necessary for this.

As for socialism, my first contact was with European, mainly British, socialism, not with the socialism of Marx and Lenin. When I started the movement towards independence, we talked of independence, not socialism, about which we had some vague ideas. This was not altogether a bad thing, I believe, because it allowed us to form our own ideas after independence and in the face of the real problems that came to us, rather than through a particular theory: hence the Arusha Declaration, which is a very simple document having two parts – one on socialism and another on self-reliance. It is not a profound theory, but a way of dealing with practical problems which arose after independence. For example, soon after independence, we realised that civil servants expected to have the right to earn rent from the houses they had built through receiving government loans. We had to explain that this was wrong and so the Arusha Declaration says that everyone should work for his or her living. This causes a lot of trouble but it is very simple and still very relevant.

The principle of self-reliance came in response to the fact that, after independence, our members of Parliament began demanding money all the time. This was clearly an impossible demand – we all have to depend on ourselves everywhere – in the regions and the villages. So we decided to formulate the need for self-reliance as a principle. So I have nothing to change here – the need for self-reliance at all levels has never been more vital. What has gone wrong with the Arusha Declaration is that it is not being carried out. It remains relevant and I would not change a comma if I were to rewrite it now.

Listening to President Nyerere, I remembered the speech he gave last week at the All African Women's Conference in Arusha. This speech reflects to a great extent the fundamental ideas rooted in African culture, ideas which have always emphasised dialogue and discussion rather than mere obedience. In this speech,

Nyerere also showed the links that exist between the three problems of an unjust international economic system, of poverty and of the exploitation of women. He underlined the fact that every oppressed group in history has obtained its freedom through its own will and efforts. And so the African woman will have to liberate herself through her own struggle, just as the Third World must fight for its own economic emancipation.

After the Arusha meeting, I returned to Dar es Salaam where I began to hear that Nyerere was planning to resign as president next year and to devote himself to leading the party, CCM, and so I asked him about this.

Nyerere: It is true I am going. I am not very old – I am 62 – but that is not the point. The point is that I have been leading my country since the beginning of the struggle for independence 30 years ago and since the union with Zanzibar 20 years ago. So I think by now I have probably done all that I can do to help my country. One could go on but I do not believe that 'going on' is the issue. It is so much more important to look at the future, to begin to look forward to a new leadership to deal with the new problems. I was not even intending to stand as president at the last elections in 1980, so I said publicly then that the 1980–85 term would be final. There is a lot of pressure on me but I believe I have to help Tanzania to look to the future and to get away from the fear of 'what happens'. I do not like this fear. My enemies and the enemies of Tanzania want me to go because then every thing will stop: the socialism, the unity, the liberation. This is nonsense. I would want to retire if only to prove them wrong! But next year I believe I should take one step back and remain chairman of CCM until 1987. I believe a younger person should take over as head of state.

Nyerere has said elsewhere that a strong party is important because it is in this way that people can take part in achieving social justice and development. We all have the right to this but history shows that it is not enough to have the right; we must also have the power to exercise our rights, the power that comes only through unity and continuous resistance.

In the plane going back to Cairo, I felt so optimistic. I saw the Nile extending from its source in the heart of Africa to reach

Egypt, the African-Arab state. And on the horizon of the 1980s I saw our hopes extend, the hope of Egypt returning to her rightful place in the heart of the Arab world – and Africa.

Originally published in the Egyptian weekly magazine El Mussawar, *Cairo, 19 October 1984. English translation by Dr El Saadawi.*

Note

1. In 1981, the Reagan administration invented the policy of 'constructive engagement' with South Africa ostensibly to end its isolation and to persuade its racist leadership to begin reforming apartheid. In reality, this was a cover for the real aim, which was to legitimise US–western support for the South African government in arms, military personnel and financial aid in support of its campaign of destabilisation in southern Africa, to break the unity of the Frontline Sates and to roll back the Marxist governments of Maozambique and Angola. Mozambique under President Samora Machel was alone in taking US policy at face value and was persuaded to sign a bilateral non-aggression pact with South Africa in March 1984, much to the shock and dismay of the ANC, which was expelled from Maputo at South Africa's demand, and of the Frontline Sates. This pact did not last long and the Frontline States re-affirmed their unity and their solidarity behind Mozambique.

Annar Cassam comments on Nyerere's *El Mussawar* interview

Our generation was a generation of nationalists struggling for the independence of our own countries – that is what we were there for.

Cassam: The interviewer herself places him within the first generation of founding leaders of the Third World and the non-aligned countries such as Nkrumah, Nasser, Nehru and Tito. These were the men who emerged as the European empires crashed all over the globe and a host of freedom-fighters and nation-builders worked to pick up the pieces and re-anchor their separate and varied countries into two new and unifying networks at the Organisation of African Unity (OAU) and the Non-Aligned Movement (NAM).

In Africa Nyerere, alone of his generation of nationalists, ran the full race and stayed the course; he alone never forgot what he was there for. He alone could say 30 years later, at the moment of his choosing, that he had done what had to be done and it was time he and the country moved on. These were three decades during which many of his contemporaries lost their way (Nkrumah and Kenyatta), were assassinated (Lumumba and Mboya), or whose health and careers were broken in their own homelands (Nasser and Ben Bella).

The plight of the Palestinians is very different and much worse. When we were fighting for our independence, I was in Tanganyika, Kenyatta was in Kenya ... But the Palestinians have been deprived of their own country...

Cassam: In the 60 years since the creation of Israel on dispossessed Palestinian land, this basic fact is the one reality that has yet to be faced by the 'international community', including Barack Obama. The idea that a 'two-state solution' can be magically fashioned out of the rubble of biblically inspired colonisation and military occupation is a costly miscalculation based on an erroneous diagnosis of the Palestinian–Israeli tragedy. As Mahatma Gandhi put it in 1938, 'A religious act cannot be performed with the aid of the bayonet and the bomb.'

The Arab countries, however, would be wrong in thinking their separate freedoms (and oil wealth) are secure while their Palestinian brothers and neighbours live in danger of extinction. And this same logic, which Nkrumah pronounced and Nyerere applied to the African liberation struggle, will ensure that even when every Palestinian has been hounded out of every inch of occupied territory, the Middle East will still not attain peace and stability.

I believe very strongly in unity. Sometimes, I am accused of supporting unity for its own sake, but I believe unity is an instrument of liberation.

Cassam: This is the central pillar of his belief, his view of the world and of his strategy for change. The idea of unity is not sentimentally exclusive, nor is it merely a political slogan. For Nyerere, it was what he was and what we are, 'a part of each other'. In this interview, the context is the altercation between himself, on the one hand, and Nasser and Nkrumah, on the other, who both became very 'impatient' with the 'reactionaries' (who shall remain nameless) at the OAU in those early years. By the same token, he then defended Egypt from being expelled from the OAU (and later from the NAM) when Sadat 'went too far' at Camp David in 1979. And in defending Egypt, he was protecting the unity of the OAU because the 'oppressed must not give up their unity – only the enemy can rejoice at its loss'.

Later in this interview, he explains another dimension of the meaning of the unity principle when describing the stages and the reasoning that led to one-party democracy within the Tanganyika African National Union (TANU). This development not only brought about democracy and debate in the country, it also brought unity, one of Tanzania's major strengths, for 'it allowed the party to articulate the reasonable aspirations of the majority of our people'.

This almost instinctive drive for unity enabled him to forge the Tanzanian nation and identity out of 127 tribes and different racial and religious affiliations very soon after independence. It was the strategic imperative guiding his initiatives at the OAU and elsewhere on behalf of the liberation struggles of southern and South Africa. It was manifest in his leadership of the Frontline States and of the different historical, linguistic, political, administrative and economic characteristics of countries such as Zambia, Mozambique, Angola, Zimbabwe, Namibia and Botswana, which he later forged into the Southern African Development Community (SADC).

It is true I am going. I am not very old – I am 62 – but that is not the point. The point is that I have been leading my country since the beginning of the struggle for independence 30 years ago and since the Union with Zanzibar 20 years ago. So I think by now I have probably done all that I can do to help my country. One could go on but I do not believe that 'going on' is the issue. It is so much more important to look to the future...

Cassam: Mwalimu had to abandon his first attempt at retiring at the end of his presidential mandate for 1975–80. The country was not ready for it in 1980 and was shocked by the very idea.

Mwalimu realised this and so stayed for another five years, giving plenty of prior notice and reassuring the nation there was no need to fear his departure.

On the eve of his retirement, in November 1985, he thanked the 3,000 CCM delegates and all citizens at the farewell meeting at the Diamond Jubilee Hall for 'having made Tanzania what it is today. Together, we have built a Nation. What more can I say?'

Reading history backwards with Mwalimu

Seithy Chachage

In an interview in the early 1970s, looking back on the events of the 1960s, Mwalimu Julius Kambarage Nyerere said that he usually viewed earlier events in the light of what he had learned recently: 'If there is something I don't understand,' he told the interviewer, 'I begin to read history backwards' (Smith 1973, p. 191). Mwalimu Nyerere understood that history can tell us something about the present; that people learn from the past.

Mwalimu Nyerere was a teacher of biology and history at St Mary's College in Tabora after completing his studies at Makerere in 1945, with a diploma in education. By this time, he had already acquainted himself with some philosophical works that sharpened his ideas and thinking in general. He had already read even the essays of the British economist-philosopher, 'John Stuart Mill, on representative government and on the subjugation of women', which had a great influence on him (Smith 1973, p. 47).[1] At Edinburgh University, where he graduated in 1952, Mwalimu Nyerere had studied history, economics and philosophy.

Mwalimu Nyerere, therefore understood very well that 'although the past does not change, the present does; each generation asks questions of the past, and finds new areas of sympathy as it relives different aspects of the past' (Hill 1978, p. 15). It was within the spirit which was succinctly summarised by Michael Banton (1977, p. 3): 'people interpret their own time in the light of their beliefs about the past, and if they misunderstand the past they cannot properly understand the present. In human affairs there is a continuous interrelation between the present and the past...'

19

On the Necessity of History

If history is important, the basic questions that befuddle one when examining the present are: How do we stand in regard to the past? What are the relations between the past, present and future? What have we actually learnt from the past experience of attempts to build a free and egalitarian society, which is self-reliant? Does the past still stand as a model for the present and the future?

Is there anything like wisdom that was represented by Mwalimu Nyerere, which can be considered to be part of a collective memory of how things were and should be done and therefore ought to be done? In sum what have we learnt from the past in the course of adopting neoliberal policies since the late 1980s apart from feeling proud or celebrating some arbitrary choice of landmarks such as 'unity and togetherness' or what we consider to be the 'good' heritage left by the Father of the Nation?

Obviously, although the present is an offshoot of the past, it stands quite far apart from it. It was the problems of development and equity that preoccupied Nyerere throughout his life. The recognition that the country's majority were rural dwellers made him concentrate on rural development – a term almost unheard of in contemporary political and economic discourse. As a leader, he had respect for Spartan living that took frugality seriously and consciously because he stood for the defence of the poor and the marginalised.

In his thinking then, corruption was one of the biggest dangers at the top. He considered it to be 'the silent scramble for Africa. Make yourself rich as quickly as possible!' This was not desirable: 'But the big scramble for personal wealth in Africa is not going to help. There is not enough wealth on this continent. It will all be at the top, and the people will be left with nothing' (Smith 1973, p. 22).

The End of Poverty

The 1960s and early 1970s were years of high enthusiasm, optimism, hopes and dreams of a bright future society devoid of all forms of arbitrariness, domination, exploitation, oppression, etc, unlike contemporary times when we are invited, day in day out, to celebrate the present as the best of all possible worlds. Many of the concepts in circulation then that described the unequal relations between the Mammonites[2] and Lazaruses[3] of this world, and rebellions against such relations, are not chic in contemporary times. Most of us shirk from using them for fear of being labelled politically incorrect or at worst, mavericks, old-fashioned or dinosaurs.[4] In those times, statements such as the following, made by Mwalimu Julius Nyerere to the Maryknoll Sisters in New York on 10 October 1970, were simple and straightforward:

> Poverty is not the real problem of the modern world. For we have the knowledge and resources which would enable us to overcome poverty. The real problem – the thing which creates misery, wars and hatred among men – is the division of mankind into rich and poor.
>
> We can see this division at two levels. Within nation states there are a few individuals who have great wealth and whose wealth gives them great power; but the vast majority of the people suffer every degree of poverty and deprivation...
>
> And looking at the world as a collection of nation states, we see the same pattern repeated. There are a few wealthy nations which dominate the whole world economically, and therefore politically; and a mass of smaller and poor nations whose destiny, it appears, is to be dominated.
>
> (Nyerere 1974, p. 82)

Such erudition and elucidation! The contemporary 'conceptualisation' of poverty, its history, causes and remedies, is done imprudently, lacking organic links with the accumulated knowledge and experiences of our societies. People from Iringa have an adage which goes: '*Ikitele ikilovela sa kisunga kikavaandikilwa*' – 'An old pot may be used again to keep milk.' This ancient wisdom has been completely buried today.

The people's enemies then were conceptualised in terms of poverty, disease and ignorance, resulting from historically evolved forms of inequalities, domination and exploitation. Then it was understood that the poor were poor because they were exploited, powerless, dominated, persecuted and marginalised, while the rich were rich because they lived off the sweat of others. That is, human constructed social economic relations induced poverty for the majority of the people, while enriching a few.

In practice during that period, the assault on poverty was premised on the belief that poverty eradication was possible.[5]

It was believed that democracy as a practice was more or less linked to the whole question of poverty eradication and access and control of productive resources. It was democracy rather than simply the existence of a multiparty system and the political parties' competition for state power that would enable people's self-reproduction socially as well as ensure more equal and equitable social development.

In those years, the contemporary mythology of what is now fashionable – globalisation – was explained in terms of a world system of capitalist relations, which had become more interlinked than ever before as a result of the communication and technological revolutions. But for Mwalimu Nyerere and those who stood for emancipatory modes of politics, nationally and continentally, this resulted in an intensification of exploitative relations. Rather than the emergence of one world the process was resulting in the fragmentation of the world nationally and internationally between the poor and the rich – the former being the majority and the latter the minority. In his words:

> The world is one in technological terms. Men have looked down on the Earth and seen its unity. In jet planes I can travel from Tanzania to New York in a matter of hours. Radio waves enable us to talk to each other – either in love or abuse – without more than a few seconds elapsing between our speech and the hearing of it. Goods are made which include materials and skills from all over the world – and are then put on sale thousands of miles from their place of manufacture.
>
> Yet at the same time as interdependence of man is increased through advance of technology, the divisions between men also increase at an ever increasing rate ... So the world is not one. Its people are more divided now, and also more conscious of their divisions, than they have ever been. They are divided between those who are satiated and those who are hungry. They are divided between those with power and those without power. They are divided between those who dominate and those who are dominated; between those who exploit and those who are exploited.
>
> (Nyerere 1974, pp. 86–7)

For him, 'Free enterprise' between dwarfs and giants was considered to be an illusion. 'Injustice and peace are in the long run incompatible; stability in a changing world must mean ordered change towards justice, not mechanical respect for the status quo' (Nyerere 1974, p. 84). In 1977, he was to explain to the press in Atlanta (USA) that what was needed to overcome poverty was 'a system of trade which does not have a built-in mechanism that transfers wealth from the poor to the rich. This is what happens now. At present, there is a built-in mechanism which transfers wealth from the poor to the rich. We want this changed'.

Rather than 'governance' (that is to govern or rule and not to lead), as is fashionable now, in those times, the prerequisite for development was people, land, good policies and good leadership (Nyerere 1968, p. 243). Mwalimu Nyerere told the Maryknoll Sisters that development had to be accompanied by equitable distribution of wealth. It was not 'simply an increase in the national income figures of the poor countries, nor listing of the huge increases in the production of this or that industry,' new roads, factories, farms, etc. Though these were quite essential, they were not enough in themselves.

> The economic growth must be of such a kind, and so organised, that it benefits the nations and the peoples who are now suffering from poverty. This means that social and political development must go alongside economic development – or even precede it. For unless society is so organised that the people control their own economies and their own economic activity, then economic growth will result in increased injustice because it will lead to inequality both nationally and internationally … Political independence is meaningless if a nation does not control the means by which its citizens can earn their living.
>
> (Nyerere 1968, p. 88)

For Mwalimu Nyerere, societies were supposed to be organised in such a way that they served 'social justice in what has been called the "revolution of rising expectations"'.

In the pre-liberalisation years, the government committed its resources in the service of ordinary working people. In practice, the government used to collect taxes for the purposes of public provision of social and developmental services in a bid to reduce the gap between the rich and the poor and fight against poverty, disease and ignorance. Thus, by 1982, there were schools in virtually all villages in the country and all children – whether poor or

23

rich – were going to school through a universal primary education programme on public financing.

More significant was the fact that more than 95 per cent of
adults could read and write due to literacy campaigns that had
been conducted over the years. Even medical services were
being provided through public financing. There were no landless
rural dwellers either, to speak of. These were not 'free services'
as claimed by the ideologues of the current dispensation who
champion the virtues of private provisioning of such services:
these were paid for collectively through taxation. It is such policies that were the real foundation of Tanzania's unity, peace and
togetherness.

The post-independence government took over the provision
of education, health and other social and economic services. The
post-independence state became the sphere of moral 'universal-
ism'; with a development model which tended towards economic
development and social welfare policies. It was money from
taxation that paid for the services – social and developmental. It
was the poor who were being protected and not the rich and the
powerful (the 'investors') as happens now.

As Mwalimu Nyerere again pointed out to the press in Atlanta
(USA) in 1977, 'You can't end poverty through charity. Within
a single nation, you don't end poverty through charity. You get
people to work, you allow them to work, you get jobs for them,
you get them trained and they work ... You tax people,' he illus-
trated. 'Even in this country where I think the gap between the
rich and the poor is very large,' he further observed, 'you still tax
the rich more in order that you may get money ... But I'm saying
the theory is accepted, that the rich are taxed in order that you
may try to reduce the gap between the poor and the rich. They are
taxed. They are not asked to pay voluntarily.'

Back to the Future

Within the attempts to build an egalitarian society, Mwalimu
Nyerere then championed the position that Tanzania's identity
was Africa. In the early 1970s, when asked about what sort of a
country he expected Tanzania to be in 20 years time, he answered:
'I hope there won't be a Tanzania. If there is not an Africa, then

at least I hope there will be an East Africa. But if we have failed to use African nationalism; if we have failed to take another step toward Pan-Africanism during that period; we should at least have a Tanzania that is committed to Pan-Africanism itself.' He summed up: 'And by that time we should have a society of which the people are very proud; we should really have built a classless society. So, if there should still be a Tanzania 20 years from now, I hope it will be a classless society very committed to an African goal' (Smith, 1973, p. 202–3).

Such simple clarity is currently almost completely lacking. In contemporary times, a new mode of logic is hammered into our heads: *'Mtaji wa maskini nguvu zake mwenyewe'* (the poor person's capital is his/her own efforts or, put in other words, the poor are poor because they are work-shy, and thus a problem for the rest of the society, since they cannot budget, save and invest). From this viewpoint, the problem with the poor is that they have low intelligence and will always be with us: thus the talk is all about poverty alleviation instead of eradication, as it was in the past. The underlying assumption is that there are individualist solutions to the problem of poverty, couched in terms of competence, rational calculations and efficiency, within which there are winners and losers – nationally, regionally or internationally.

Within this context, dazzling statistics about the 'progress of the country', despite the unravelled investment rates – foreign and local – in commerce, trading, import and export trade, mining, tourism, fishery, natural resources, etc, are eloquently quoted to discredit some of the past experiences that sought to promote egalitarian social relations. In sum, economic growth has taken precedence over everything else, the degeneration of the population and the misery of the working people, as a result of exploitation, slave wages, exploitative terms of trade for rural produce, the alienation of land and the expropriation of natural and mineral resources, which has increased over the years notwithstanding.

It is claimed that it is economics and not politics which determines everything in the contemporary world, since the cold war is over and the world has become one. Thus even Pan-Africanism is dead: fellow Africans from other countries are considered foreigners, or some of those who have been living in the country for many years are declared non-citizens.

Today, we are involved in the celebration of the present, an era in which not production but the markets and stock exchanges are the determining aspect of social life. It is an era when it is said it is possible for the state to withdraw from social provisioning since the market can fill the vacuum created by its withdrawal. To the extent that markets can create conditions for development and human welfare, the state in its current form can only confine itself to the management of law and order.

In this regard, it no longer requires social policies to legitimise itself, as it did previously. Rather than the state playing statistics, it is now the upper class doing so, while the middle class play the stock market and the lower classes await for fortunes from bingo and beauty contests: the best person wins.

These aspects of the past are worth an examination in their own right. What we urgently require are historical forms of knowledge that can arm Tanzanians and Africans in general to intervene in the present circumstances, which are marginalising the majority of the people on an ever-increasing scale. We are living in a period marked by the failure of most of us to think about or even conceptualise the historical possibilities of social transformations in terms of how to achieve a stage of society where a man or a woman's humanity is not contested. The human desire to live a life devoid of all forms of arbitrariness – whether class, gender, race, communal exclusivity, etc – is no longer problematised; it is taken for granted. Many of us have given up all struggles to search for alternative policy solutions and truths that would lead to the construction of humane communities.

This chapter is extracted from the introduction to Seithy Chachage's forthcoming book Against Historical Amnesia and Collective Imbecility: Essays on Tanzania's Contemporary Transformations.

Notes

1. The essay 'The Subjection of Women', first published in 1869 under J.S. Mill's name, was actually written by his wife, Harriet Taylor, which is illustrative of the circumstances under which women found themselves when it came to publishing unconventional ideas.
2. False gods of riches. From the false god of riches and avarice, Mammon. Riches regarded as an object of worship and greedy pursuit; wealth as an evil, more or less personified. In Matthew 6: 24 it is stated: 'Ye cannot serve God and mammon.'

3. The diseased beggar in Jesus' parable of the rich man and the beggar (Luke 16: 19–31).

4. Historically, dinosaurs may be extinct, but in science fiction fables, such as the movie *Jurassic Park*, these come back with a vengeance. It may be a fable, but the truth is usually that the ghosts of the past haunt the minds of the living like a nightmare, hence such fables.

5. Earlier on in February 1967, Nyerere had declared in combative and militant language that 'TANU is in a war against poverty and oppression in our country; this struggle is aimed at moving the people of Tanzania (and the people of Africa as whole) from a state of poverty to a state of prosperity.' Then followed the famous, scintillating words which were an inspiration in those days: 'We have been oppressed a great deal, we have been exploited a great deal and we have been disregarded a great deal. It is our weakness that has led to our being oppressed, exploited and disregarded. Now we want a revolution – a revolution which brings to an end our weakness, so that we are never exploited, oppressed, or humiliated' (Nyerere 1968, p. 235).

References

Banton, Michael (1977) *The Idea of Race*, London, Tavistock Publications

Hill, Christopher (1978) *The World Turned Upside Down*, Aylesbury, Penguin

Nyerere, Julius K. (1968) *Freedom and Socialism*, Nairobi, Oxford University Press

Nyerere, Julius K. (1974) *Man and Development*, Nairobi, Oxford University Press

Smith, William E. (1973) *Nyerere of Tanzania*, Nairobi, TransAfrica Publishers

Mwalimu Julius Nyerere: an intellectual in power

Haroub Othman

This is the text of the first Mwalimu Nyerere Memorial Lecture
which was delivered by Haroub Othman on 14 October
2005 at the University of Cape Town, South Africa.

I want first of all to thank the East African Students Society, and
the University of Cape Town in general, for organising this occasion to commemorate the death of Mwalimu Julius Nyerere,
and for inviting me to give this lecture on someone I very much
respect and admire. In my life I have met many African leaders; to
mention a few, and in order not to cause offence, only dead ones
– Kwame Nkrumah of Ghana, Ahmed Sékou Touré of Guinea,
Ferhat Abbas of Algeria, Augustinho Neto of Angola, Samora
Machel of Mozambique, Amilcar Cabral of Guinea Bissau and
Cape Verde and Oginga Odinga of Kenya. I have also met several
South African leaders, including historic personalities such as
Oliver Tambo, Yusuf Dadoo, Walter Sisulu, Govan Mbeki, Alfred
Nzo, Duma Nokwe and Joe Slovo. But Mwalimu Nyerere was not
just a leader; he was a statesman. I have deliberately avoided calling him a politician, because politicians come and go. Statesmen
live on – the impact of their presence in society is felt for many
years after their death. If I can paraphrase William Shakespeare,
the good they do lives after them. I found Mwalimu Nyerere to be
most articulate, supremely good at putting complex issues in very
simple language and very effective in relating to his audience.

   Many definitions have been rendered as to who is an intellectual. Is it somebody who has been to a university or, as Ali
Mazrui once put it, 'one who is excited by ideas and has acquired

the ability to handle some of these ideas effectively'? Is it a professional or one who can stand up and talk on Picasso, Leo Tolstoy
or Beethoven? Byron considered an intellectual not only a person
attracted to ideas, but whose purpose in life, whose thoughts and
actions were determined by those ideas. Issa Shivji holds that one
of the important attributes of an intellectual is 'the ability to laugh
at ourselves'. I consider an intellectual as not only a person who
is able to analyse the present but is also able to articulate ideas
that would have a lasting impact on those who receive them. But
whatever definition one might adopt, of importance is the fact
that the role of an intellectual in any society is enormous.

Western education in Africa, especially in southern Africa, is
a recent phenomenon. Pre-colonial African societies, with few
exceptions, had no formal educational systems. But if the purpose
of any education, as Julius Nyerere put it, 'is to transmit from one
generation to the next the accumulated wisdom and knowledge
of the society, and to prepare the young people for their future
membership of the society and their active participation in its
maintenance and development', then these societies had appropriate educational systems. The aim of western education, which
came with colonialism, was to instil in the minds of its recipients
an idolisation for the superiority of the colonial master. First it
was the sons of chiefs and other traditional leaders that received
this education; and later, with the expansion of the colonial
economy, more and more people acquired it. Budo, Kisubi, Fort
Hare, Makerere, were all created for that purpose. The aim was
to produce clerks, teachers, priests, agricultural extension workers, hospital assistants, and others to help in the running of the
colonial machinery.

University education was restricted to only a few. It was only
after independence that education became accessible to more
people. Of the few that received western education, not all acted
according to the expectations of the colonial regime. Some turned
out to be the most vehement opponents of the colonial system not
only in the political and economic spheres, but also in education,
culture and other areas. The reasons are obvious.

Colonialism affected both the traditional chief and the ordinary
worker. It did not even allow the emergence of the native capitalist. While in the colonial possessions of Asia and semi-colonial

China, a local compradorial class was allowed to exist, in most of Africa this class did not emerge. It is no wonder then that in most of the African states the harbingers of the nationalist movements were people coming from the colonial bureaucracy.

The countries of southern Africa are not a homogeneous group. There are differences in history, culture and experiences. Even those that were ruled by the same colonial power, such as Zimbabwe and Tanzania, or Angola and Mozambique, have differences in their social compositions and levels of economic development. There are amongst them countries that achieved independence peacefully, such as Tanzania and Swaziland, and others, like Mozambique, Angola and Zimbabwe, which attained it through the barrel of a gun.

Due to the specific conditions of the countries of the region, each one traversed the independence path in its own way. And each country brought to the fore of the independence movements a group of individuals who by any definition can be called intellectuals. What was common in almost all the countries is the fact that this group comprised people with the highest commitment to the ideals of independence and dedication to their achievement.

The backgrounds of this highly politically active intelligentsia vary. In the case of mainland Tanzania, whose economy was basically peasant-based and where education in the early colonial days was mostly provided by Christian missionary schools, the products of such a set-up were people whose vision did not go beyond the peasant collective. This was different from a place such as South Africa where a large section of the community had been uprooted from their land, a numerically strong working class had been formed and where an independent political organisation of this class existed. The logical tendency in this kind of situation would be to produce intellectuals who, to quote Amilcar Cabral, would know where the struggle for national independence ends and the struggle for social emancipation begins.

One of the successes of the colonial system in the region was that it was able to produce an academia that was dependent on western intellectual production. This intelligentsia understood what was taking place in other societies, but lacked adequate knowledge of its own societies. This is what prevailed for a very long time in the African universities. Admittedly, a few individuals were to be found in the universities who went against the general mould, but the pattern was for the universities to be replicas of their western peers. As Mwalimu Nyerere stated, 'Our universities have aimed at understanding western society, and being understood by western society, apparently assuming that by this means they were preparing their students to be – and themselves being – of service to African society'. The University of Dar es Salaam was the first in the region to break out of this mould.

Founded in 1961 as a constituent college of the University of East Africa (itself enjoying cooperative status with the University of London), the University College of Dar es Salaam became a full university in 1970 when a decision was taken by the three East African states to each form its own national university. The University of Dar es Salaam in its curricula and research agenda tried to break away from the paradigms set up by others. It aimed at inculcating a sense of commitment to society, and tried to make all who came into contact with it accept the new values appropriate to the post-colonial society. There was a deliberate attempt to fight intellectual arrogance because it was felt that such arrogance had no place in a society of equal citizens.

The University of Dar es Salaam also played its part in the intellectual development of the region. In the 10-year period from 1967 to 1977, the university was a major cooking pot of ideas, and provided a splendid platform for debate and discussion. No African scholar, leader or freedom fighter could ignore its environs. While the government brought its official guests to see its picturesque, Mount Olympus-like exterior, others came to seek knowledge or refine their ideological positions. Here, the East and West Germans, who officially were not talking to each other; the Chinese and the Americans, who officially could not stand each other; and the white and black South Africans, who at home could not even sit together in the same church, met in the seminar rooms built by the Swedes and the British to debate not only Tanzania's development path but also the Vietnam war, the Palestinian question, apartheid, the Chinese cultural revolution and countless other subjects. Very intense were these debates, and a huge number of discourses and manuscripts were churned out.

That kind of atmosphere existed partly due to conditions created by the Arusha Declaration – the country's policy document on socialism and self-reliance – and partly due to the liberal-minded-ness of Mwalimu Julius Nyerere, who was the university college's 'visitor', and after the establishment of the University of Dar es Salaam, its first chancellor. But one must also not underestimate the impact that the presence of the liberation movements had on Tanzania's intellectual development. These movements were not only engaged in struggles in their respective countries, but their leading cadres, as a result of these struggles, were forced to con-stantly refine their theories and assumptions; and they found the university campus an excellent testing ground for that exercise. Thus, during the course of this process, the liberation move-ments not only brought in their towering figures, but also their dissidents and the harbingers of future conflicts. From Frelimo of Mozambique came people like the religio-tribalist Rev Urio Simango, the liberal-minded nationalist Dr Eduardo Mondlane, and the Marxist poet Marcelino dos Santos; from the ANC of South Africa, people like Duma Nokwe, Joe Jele and Ambrose Makiwane; PAC brought Lebalo and Gora Ebrahim; and the MPLA of Angola, Agostinho Neto and the future Nito Alves ele-ments. The Communist Party of South Africa brought in its tower-ing giants, Yusuf Daddoo, Moses Mabhida and Joe Slovo. Since I am in Cape Town, I should also mention that the Unity Movement also had its people appearing on the Dar es Salaam campus. Some of the most significant statements of these movements were made at the University Hill, including the famous one by Neto in 1974, before Angola's independence, on 'Who is the Enemy?' that has remained to this day the MPLA's weightiest document.

Sometime the staff houses on campus were turned into semi-nar rooms or places for social interaction. There were even times when they were used as hideouts when some leaders of liberation movements did not want their presence in the country publicly known. I remember occasions when Yusuf Dadoo and Joe Slovo (and if my memory does not fail me, Thabo Mbeki, the present president of South Africa, too) came to the university to 'reflect'.

The Tanzanian press at the time provided a very useful plat-form for debate and discussion. *The Nationalist* (the ruling party's paper) was under the editorship of Benjamin Mkapa, the current president of Tanzania [from 1995 to 2005]; and the government newspaper, *The Standard*, was under the headship of Dr Frene

Ginwala (the former speaker of the South African Parliament), as managing editor and Mwalimu Nyerere was the editor-in-chief. Apart from providing the news, these newspapers also published articles of high quality, and opened their pages for serious debates on both internal and international issues.

People from different parts of the world came to teach at Dar es Salaam. They came for different reasons. There were some who simply needed an African experience, but in a surrounding appeasing to their consciences; there were others who were moved by the country's revolutionary potential, and being internationalists, felt that they needed to contribute; and still others, taking pauses from their own struggles, needed breathing space and periods of reflection. It was definitely the most international university one could ever find in the Third World. Some of the people who came were directly from school themselves and therefore Dar es Salaam constituted their 'baptism'; others were accomplished academics of international renown. Names of South Africans that easily come to mind are those of Ruth First, Archie Mafeje, Denis Brutus, Willy Kogkositle (the former husband of the present speaker of the South African parliament), Harold Wolpe, Bob Leshoai, Sixghashe, Dan O'Meara and his former wife, Linzi Manicom, and Tshabalala (the former husband of the present South Africa minister for health).

From within the eastern and southern Africa region, there came Nathan Shamuyarira, who later became foreign minister of Zimbabwe; Ibbo Mandaza, Miti and Frank Mbengo, all also from Zimbabwe; Orton Chirwa, the first justice minister of Malawi, and his wife, Vera (now a member of the African Commission for Human and People's Rights) and Mutharika, the brother of the present Malawian president; Tunguru Huaraka from Namibia; Mahmood Mamdani (who is known to this university), Yash Tandon and Dan Nabudere from Uganda; and Yash Ghai from Kenya. But people came also from far flung areas, including Guyanese historian and political activist Walter Rodney; the Hungarian economist Tamás Szentes; the Nigerian political scientists Okidigbo Nnoli and Claude Ake; the Ghanaians Aki Sawyer and Emanuel Hansen; the British historians Terence Ranger and John Illiffe, political scientist Lionel Cliffe and economists John Loxley and Peter Lawrence; the Canadians – Cranford Pratt who in fact was the first principal of the university college and political scientist John Saul; and many others from Denmark, the United States and other shores. When I was in the then German Democratic Republic in 1985 for a conference on African studies, I found out that many of their Africa specialists had been to Dar es Salaam.

Many people, like Boutros Boutros Ghali, who was a university professor before he became a minister in Egypt and later on the first African secretary general of the UN, and Adebayo Adedeji, the former executive secretary of the UN Economic Commission for Africa, included a stopover at the University Hill in their schedule whenever they happened to be in Dar es Salaam. Yoweri Museveni, a few months before he marched into Kampala, went to the university campus to see his old friends; and on his first state visit to Tanzania, he went to deliver a public lecture at the university. The Rivonia heroes, after their release from Robben Island prison, passed through Dar es Salaam on their way to Sweden to meet Oliver Tambo, and they came to the university to talk to the community.

Many academics have achieved fame from intellectual works they produced while in Dar es Salaam. Walter Rodney's legendary book, *How Europe Underdeveloped Africa*, that of Clive Thomas, *On Problems of Transition*, and Tamás Szentes' classic, *The Political Economy of Underdevelopment*, were all written in Dar es Salaam. The university was not only a haven for radical scholars and activists; the students also found it an exciting and productive experience. Issa Shivji, in his student days, had already produced *Tanzania: The Silent Class Struggle*; and the current President of Uganda, Yoweri Museveni, Kapote Mwakasungura, who later became Malawian high commissioner to Zimbabwe, Salim Msoma, the present principal secretary in the Tanzania Ministry of Transport and Communication, and Andrew Shija, who after graduation joined the Tanzania army, left their classrooms and joined Frelimo cadres in the liberated areas of Portuguese-ruled Mozambique. John Saul, when teaching at the University of Dar es Salaam, did the same thing. The students' journal, *Cheche* [The Spark], subsequently *Maji Maji*, was very much sought after, and the teaching staff vied with each other to have their articles published in it.

From its inception in 1961 as a university college until 1985 when he stepped down as the chancellor, Mwalimu Nyerere played an important role in the shaping of the university, and took a keen personal interest in its intellectual development. I do not think there was any national institution that he visited as often as the university.

Mwalimu Nyerere was born on 13 April 1922 in the small village of Butiama among a minority ethnic group in Tanzania. He grew up in typical African village surroundings, and later on in life became the embodiment of the African struggle for freedom and national independence and a symbol of people's aspirations for social emancipation and human fulfilment. It was at the age of 12 that he started going to school, and only after coming of age was he confirmed to Christianity. From Tabora school, at the time the citadel of education in what was called Tanganyika, he proceeded to Makerere College in Uganda to acquire a diploma in education. Makerere was at that time the highest institution of learning in East Africa, and constituted an important period for Mwalimu Nyerere in formulating the objectives and principles that guided him later on in his life. After he left Makerere, he stated:

> While I was at Makerere I understood that my Government was spending annually something in the neighbourhood of 80 pounds on my behalf. But that did not mean very much to me: after all, 80 pounds is only a minute fraction of the total amount which is collected every year from the African tax-payers. But today that 80 pounds has grown to mean a very great deal to me. It is not only a precious gift but a debt that I can never repay.
>
> I wonder whether it has ever occurred to many of us that while that 80 pounds was being spent on me (or for that matter on any of the past or present students of Makerere) some village dispensary was not being built in my village or some other village. People may actually have died through lack of medicine merely because eighty pounds which could have been spent on a fine village dispensary was spent on me, a mere individual, instead. Because of my presence at the college (and I did nothing to deserve Makerere) many Aggreys and Booker Washingtons remained illiterate for lack of a school to which they could go because the money which could have gone towards building a school was spent on Nyerere, a rather foolish and irresponsible student at Makerere. My presence at

the college therefore deprived the community of the services of all those who might have been trained at those schools, and who might have become Aggreys or Booker Washingtons. How can I repay this debt to the community? ... The community spends all that money upon us because it wants us as lifting levers, and as such we must remain below and bear the whole weight of the masses to be lifted, and we must facilitate that task of lifting.

From Makerere, Mwalimu Nyerere taught briefly before he proceeded to do a master's degree in history at the University of Edinburgh in Scotland. He was the first Tanganyika African to acquire an overseas degree. It was in Edinburgh that his political ideas were crystallised.

Upon his return to Tanganyika he taught for some time in the Christian Mission schools before he threw himself fully into the nationalist struggle for independence. The Tanganyika African Association (TAA), founded in 1929 by traders and civil servants in urban areas, was basically a social organisation. Only in 1954 did it transform into a political one and become known as the Tanganyika African National Union (TANU), with Nyerere as its president.

As I have stated, Julius Nyerere has dominated the Tanzanian political and intellectual scene for almost five decades, and even now with his death, his influence is still felt. I will try here to briefly look at some of his ideas.

In his *Ujamaa – The Basis of African Socialism*, Mwalimu Nyerere dismissed the idea that classes had existed in pre-colonial African societies, claiming instead that these societies lived in tranquillity and peace and had experienced no antagonistic contradictions. He felt that it was possible for Africans, regardless of their social backgrounds, to come together in national movements and to retain that unity after independence. He not only dismissed the notion of the existence of classes prior to colonisation but did not acknowledge their evolution during the colonial period.

In 1967 Tanzania declared its intention to build socialism on the basis of self-reliance. Julius Nyerere was definitely the intellectual power behind the Arusha Declaration. In fact the sociologist Jeanette Hartmann, who taught at the University of Dar es

Salaam, has stated that it was written by Nyerere himself, claiming that she had seen the draft in Mwalimu Nyerere's handwriting (Hodd, 1988). The declaration attracted huge attention. To social democrats in Europe it heralded the possibility of seeing the realisation of their ideals in an African set-up. Imperialist powers, on the other hand, were afraid that Tanzania would set up an example to the rest of Africa. From 1967, then, Tanzania's actions on the domestic and international arenas were judged in accordance with the terms of the Arusha Declaration. Tanzania's close relationship with China or its acceptance of aid from the then socialist countries of Eastern Europe were seen as tendencies to further integrate Tanzania within the socialist orbit. But, as Julius Nyerere kept reiterating, the Arusha Declaration should have been viewed as a statement of intent. Neither in 1967 nor in 1985 when he stepped down from the presidency was Tanzania a socialist state.

The declaration was not without flaws and its implementation was far from successful. There were reasons for this; but as a blueprint for development, it was something unique in Africa at that time. It was assertive and provided great hopes for millions of Tanzanians. In another paper – 'Socialism: the rational choice' – Mwalimu argued that for a country like Tanzania, socialism was the only choice, but even if it wanted to build capitalism, that option was closed to it.

What Mwalimu Nyerere succeeded in doing was to put socialism on the national agenda. One cannot therefore agree with Ali Mazrui and many others who say that socialism was a 'heroic failure' in Tanzania. The *Wall Street Journal* declared:

> He fused Tanzania's 120 tribes into a cohesive state, preventing tribal conflicts plaguing so much of Africa … Above all, he proved that it is possible to forge a nation whereby vicissitudes of ethnic affiliation are banished from social and political life. He created and promoted a powerful lingua franca, Swahili, which united and educated people.

He preached racial and religious tolerance. Following Mwalimu Nyerere's departure from political power, the country collapsed into the arms of the IMF and the World Bank. When he left the per capita income was US$280. In 1998, 13 years later, it was US$140;

and school enrolment plummeted to 63 per cent. Some of the progressive achievements of the Nyerere era are being eroded, but he will definitely be remembered in history as the person who raised the prospect of socialist development in Tanzania.

Tanzania's contribution to Africa's liberation is well known. Almost all the liberation movements in Africa enjoyed sanctuary in Tanzania. The Organisation of African Unity (OAU) Liberation Committee had its headquarters in Dar es Salaam from the time the OAU was established in 1963. Julius Nyerere cannot be separated from the Tanzania position. It should be remembered that as far back as 1960, when Tanganyika was not even independent, Nyerere published a pamphlet called *Barriers to Democracy* in which he castigated the white communities in Kenya, the Rhodesias and South Africa for rejecting the concept of a multiracial society based on African majority rule. Also in 1961, just before Tanganyika's independence, in an article in the London newspaper the *Observer*, Nyerere made it clear to the British government that membership of independent Tanganyika in the Commonwealth would depend on South Africa either ending apartheid or withdrawing from the Commonwealth. Apartheid South Africa decided to withdraw from the Commonwealth.

As stated before, there is no single African liberation movement that did not enjoy the support of Tanzania. Frelimo was founded in Tanzania; the ANC, after its banning in South Africa, opened its first external mission in Tanzania; and MOLINACO, MPLA, ZANU, ZAPU, PAC and many others had Tanzania's full support. In the UN Decolonisation Committee (known as the Committee of 24), Tanzania's then permanent representative to the UN, Salim Ahmed Salim, held the chairmanship for several years. In the Non-Aligned Movement, Tanzania was in the forefront in mobilising support to the liberation struggles.

Tanzania's support to the liberation movements was not only manifested in the political and diplomatic arenas but also in the material and military fields. The Tanzanian population was mobilised many times to give material support to the liberation movements. The Tanzania People's Defence Forces trained thousands of military cadres of those liberation movements which wanted that kind of support. Tanzania was used as a facility for either storing or transporting different types of goods to the liberation movements. It is a known fact that several villages along the border with Mozambique were bombed by Portuguese planes during Frelimo's struggle for independence. All this testifies to the country's firm position on the question of African liberation. But again it was Julius Nyerere who was able not only to give an intellectual basis to this position but also to effectively articulate it.

Julius Nyerere was always non-racial in his perspective, and this at times got him into conflict with his colleagues both in the ruling party and government. During the days of the struggle for Tanganyika's independence, he rejected the position of the 'Africanists' within TANU who put forward the slogan 'Africa for Africans', meaning black Africans. In 1958, at the TANU National Conference in Tabora when some leaders strongly opposed TANU's participation in the colonially-proposed tripartite elections, where the voter had to vote for three candidates from the lists of Africans, Asians and Europeans, Julius Nyerere stood firm in recommending acceptance of the proposals. This led to the 'Africanists' marching out of TANU and forming the African National Congress. It is extremely worrying that this racist monster is reappearing now in Tanzania. Some politicians in their quest for power are using the racist card, as manifested both at last May's Chimwaga Congress of the ruling party, CCM [Chama cha Mapinduzi – Party of the Revolution/Revolutionary Party], and in the on-going election campaigns. It is very unfortunate that no stern measures are being taken against this trend, thus giving the impression that the country's leadership is condoning it.

Again, after independence, when a section of the leadership of TANU and that of the trade union movement, the Tanganyika Federation of Labour (TFL), were demanding Africanisation of the civil service, Julius Nyerere was talking of Tanganyikanisation, thus giving a non-racial content to the whole idea. His commitment to African liberation stemmed not only from these anti-racist convictions but also from his strong belief that it is evil and wrong for a foreign power to colonise another people, and that it is equally wrong for a racial minority to oppress a racial majority. Mwalimu Nyerere never doubted that whites in Zimbabwe or South Africa had the same rights as their black compatriots.

Julius Nyerere believed in peaceful means in the struggle to achieve certain political ends. He tried very much during the

Tanganyika independence struggle to steer the independence movement along peaceful lines. Even at those times when the temperature was high and militants either in TANU or TFL were calling for confrontation, Julius Nyerere continued to call for restraint. When, after being convicted of libel in a colonial court, he was faced with the option of going to prison or paying a fine, he chose the latter, not so much because he did not want to be a political prisoner, but because it was felt that in his absence things might go wrong and violence might erupt.

However, when faced with a situation where all peaceful means were closed, Mwalimu Nyerere never hesitated to advocate the use of violence against an oppressive regime. A few months before Britain handed over power to the sultan's regime in Zanzibar, he appealed to the British government, through its colonial secretary, to reconsider its intention because he felt that if the situation was not rectified to allow the majority to peacefully take over power, then violence was inevitable. And on this he was right, because four weeks after independence the sultan's regime was violently overthrown by opposition parties. Again, when nationalists in Angola, Guinea-Bissau, Mozambique, Southern Rhodesia and South Africa were forced to take up arms against colonial and apartheid regimes, Mwalimu Nyerere committed both Tanzanian resources and his own personal prestige to helping the liberation movements engage in the armed struggle, and found this to be in no contradiction with his non-violence convictions.

Mwalimu Nyerere's last visit to the University of Dar es Salaam was in December 1997 when he came to take part in the international conference on Reflections on Leadership in Africa – Forty Years after Independence. The conference was in honour of his 75th birthday and was organised jointly by the Institute of Development Studies of the University of Dar es Salaam and the Mwalimu Nyerere Foundation. Nkrumah Hall at the university, with a capacity of 500 to 600 people, was full to overflowing. The organisers had expected not more than 100 people. Ministers, leaders of political parties, academics, students (even though the university was on Christmas vacation), NGO activists, foreign diplomats, media people – they were all there. It was obvious that the centre of attraction was Mwalimu Nyerere, and that they all came to see him and hear him.

After the keynote address by the Tanzania vice president, the late Dr Omar Ali Juma, Mwalimu Nyerere was asked to speak. He spoke for more than one and a half hours, entirely extempore. It was one of his best speeches, unfortunately the last one at the university. It was full of humour, but also deeply serious, thought provoking, and provided a sense of direction. The audience loved him. That speech has been produced in full in the book that I edited based on the conference papers called *Reflections on Leadership in Africa – Forty Years after Independence,* and was published in 2000 by VUB University Press in Brussels, Belgium.

In that speech, Mwalimu was making one very important point: that Africa south of the Sahara was on its own. North America, meaning the United States and Canada, had to do something to help Mexico, otherwise the Latin wanderers would simply cross over even if a steel wall were erected. The Slavs, Croatians, Czechs and others in Eastern Europe would be attracted to western Europe, and the North Africans would be interested in southern Europe. The south-east Asians would be looking to Japan. But Africans south of the Sahara had no 'uncle' to depend on. We were on our own. We have to rely on ourselves, and to cooperate among ourselves.

After the opening ceremony, the conference went into workshops. Mwalimu Nyerere was very active in the workshops where he participated, speaking with his usual lucidity in elaboration and illustration. In one session, the audience was pensive, watching him exchanging views with Issa Shivji on the land question; and at another he explained why he had to ask a group of freedom fighters to leave the country, an issue that was raised in the paper presented by a Russian scholar on African affairs, Vladimir Shubin. After one of the sessions, Mwalimu Nyerere wanted the South African academic, Patrick Bond, and a few others to come to his Msasani residence to continue the discussion. Bond had raised the issue of Afrikaner capital in the southern Africa region and the way it was behaving.

Mwalimu Nyerere's last intellectual work was the translation into Kiswahili of Plato's *The Republic.* As he was lying in bed at London's St Thomas Hospital, he went through the manuscript, made the necessary corrections and completed them before he died. Unfortunately the work has not yet been published.

Mwalimu Nyerere was not a saint (though, according to press reports, there are discussions now amongst the Catholics in his native area about asking the church to start the process of beatifying him) and he did commit a number of mistakes. But his patriotism was unmistaken, his commitment and devotion to Africa unquestionable and his integrity outstanding. His achievements were many, and leaders in Tanzania (and in Africa), present and future, will be judged according to the yardsticks set by people like Mwalimu Julius Nyerere.

At present the southern African sub-continent is facing a deep crisis – legacies of colonialism and white domination, underdevelopment, debt problems, HIV/AIDS and natural and unnatural calamities. All these pose serious challenges to the intelligentsia of the region. The intellectuals of the colonial past could have been lured to the colonial trappings but decided to join the independence movement. The present intelligentsia have nothing to lure them into the post-colonial state. Our role is to transform our societies and to give content to human dignity. One should live so that in dying one can say: I gave all my strength for the liberation of humanity.

This lecture is reproduced here by permission of Saida Yahya-Othman.

Bibliography

The original speech did not contain any citations but this bibliography provides several useful sources of information.

Hodd, Michael (ed) (1988) *Tanzania after Nyerere,* London, Pinter Publishers

Kiernan, V.G. (1969) 'Notes on the intelligentsia', *Socialist Register,* vol. 6

Lerumo, A. (1971) Fifty Fighting Years – The South African Communist Party 1921–1971, London, Inkululeko Publication

Mamdani, M. (1986) 'Our political role today: problems and prospects', UDASA Newsletter/Forum.

Mandaza, I. (1988) 'The relationship of Third World intellectuals and progressive western scholars: an African critique', Southern Africa Political and Economic Series Trust (SAPES), no. 5, February.

Miliband, R. and Panitch, L. (eds) (1990) *The Retreat of Intellectuals, Socialist Register,* London, Merlin Press

Nyerere, J.K. (1968) 'The role of universities', in Nyerere, J.K. (1965–67) *Freedom and Socialism: a Selection of Writings and Speeches,* Dar es Salaam, Oxford University Press

Nyerere, J.K. (1968) 'Education for self-reliance', in Nyerere, J.K. *Freedom and*

Socialism. A Selection from Writings & Speeches, 1965-1967, Dar es Salaam, Oxford University Press

Nyerere, J.K. (1968) 'The intellectual needs society', quoted in Schneider, Leander (2004) *Freedom and Unfreedom in Rural Development: Julius Nyerere, Ujamaa Vijijini, and Villagization*, Canadian Association of African Studies

Nyong'o, P.A. (1988) 'African intellectuals and the state', Southern Africa Political and Economic Series Trust (SAPES), no. 5, February

Othman, H. (1980) 'Homage to a committed intellectual: Jean Paul Sartre', newspaper article

Othman, H. (1983) 'Committed scholarship and the search for a progressive development path in Southern Africa', paper presented at the SADRA Congress, Maseru, Lesotho

Othman, H. (1986) 'The political legacy of Julius Nyerere', paper presented at a conference on 'Tanzania after Nyerere', SOAS, University of London

Othman, H. (1992) 'The intellectual and transformation in Southern Africa', paper presented at a conference at the University of Western Cape, South Africa

Othman, H. (2000) *Reflections on Leadership in Africa: Forty Years After Independence*, Brussels, VUB University Press

Shivji, I.G. (1986) 'Intellectual in crisis and the crisis of intellectual', UDASA Newsletter/Forum

Julius Nyerere: between state-centred and people-centred Pan-Africanism

Horace Campbell

Pan-Africanism arose as a philosophy to restore the humanity and dignity of the African person – and indeed all humans. The concept of dignity and humanity has gone through many iterations from the period of enslavement to the current period of biotechnology when corporations have given themselves the right to patent life forms. The era of genetic engineering and eugenics has been compounded by the perils of global warming. A planet in peril threatens the lives and livelihoods of literally hundreds of millions of poor people in all parts of the world. Millions of oppressed peoples have seen concretely that the health and well-being of all citizens are interconnected. Issues of health, the environment, the safety of poor women and children bring the question of dignity to a new level and bring back to the fore matters of a people-centred Pan-African movement.

Pan-Africanism as a philosophy has always been driven by the spontaneous and organised activities of African peoples. Today the struggles over access to anti-retroviral drugs for HIV/AIDS citizens by the Treatment Action Campaign of southern Africa have again refocused attention on people-centred activities in the Pan-African world. Healthcare, global warming and the pollution of rivers and communities demonstrate that African states must be engaged to serve the interests of the ordinary person. Millions are harmed by the effects of climate change. HIV/AIDS is the most serious public health problem of our times. Each year in Africa, three million people die of HIV/AIDS, a number which has devastated communities and wreaked havoc on the economies of the continent. Why AIDS continues to spread is a highly complex question that deals with the capacities of governments to meet the public health needs of their citizens.

HIV/AIDS is generally well controlled in states that have the resources to create an adequate public health infrastructure and who can put funding towards AIDS prevention and education. States which do not have the capacity to do these things, because of violence, war, institutional corruption and other factors, are generally not able to contain the spread of the disease and defend their peoples. Hence dealing with the questions of health and global warming requires state intervention, especially the intervention of governments that place the interests of their people as a priority. Pan-Africanism and dignity entails a delicate navigation of the terrain of the people and governments.

Pan-Africanism questions the very sovereignty of the state in Africa, and instead seeks to do away with artificial colonial borders. In addition, it thrives on the dynamic energies of cooperative relations between peoples of African heritage both within Africa and without. Pan-Africanism, then, is not centred on the state, although a Pan-Africanist can certainly become the head of a state, as was the case with Julius Nyerere of Tanzania.

Nyerere successfully defended the rights of the people to food, clothing and shelter while seeking to decolonise the inherited oppressive structures of the Tanzanian state. Nyerere understood that African unity was the only road for full emancipation in Africa.

Who was Julius Nyerere?

Mwalimu Julius Nyerere was a great human being who demonstrated his respect for the ordinary African and for the lives of all human beings. He stood out in the continent for his opposition to genocidal violence and he was one of the few who raised his voice loudly against the genocide in Burundi, Rwanda and the Eastern Democratic Republic of the Congo. Up to his last days, in his capacity as one of the diplomats of the Nyerere Foundation for Peace and Development, he was a peacemaker at the forefront of trying to bring peace to Burundi and to isolate the extremists on both sides who want to use militaristic means to solve social problems.

Unlike so many other leaders of the anti-colonial movements in Africa, Nyerere did not cling to power. His decision to step down as president of Tanzania in 1985 demonstrated that political leadership was not the personal possession of any individual. He went on to head up the South Commission to promote the delinking of the South from imperial domination. In the many capacities that he served in his 77 years he was always an inspiration for those struggling for justice, peace and socialist transformation. His vision of socialism and of an original African contribution to humanity touched those in US society who are in the belly of capitalism and suffer the indignities of racism, police terror, exploitation and sexism. He provided moral leadership in a continent where many leaders thought of filling their pockets and bank accounts instead of serving their people.

Pan-Africanism and the anti-colonial struggles

The Pan-African movement has been the principal agency for the self-definition of the African people in the 20th century. This movement of self-definition has been manifest both at the subjective level of race consciousness of the African peoples and at the objective level in relation to the organisational forms that Pan-Africanism has taken to elaborate freedom. It is the organised form of Pan-Africanism that is more widely known, with the written record focusing on the seven Pan-African Congresses that were held between 1900 and 1994. Julius Nyerere hosted the sixth Pan-African Congress in Tanzania in 1974. Nyerere was a champion of the liberation of Africa and hosted the Liberation Committee of the OAU in Tanzania.

In institutional terms the African Union (successor organisation to the Organisation of African Unity) is the most concrete manifestation of state-centred Pan-African aspirations. These states continue to maintain the institutions and languages of colonial powers and so the very existence of the AU is part of the long struggle of the people to transform the inherited states. The Pan-African movement has gone through many stages in the last century and for this brief analysis of Nyerere and Pan-Africanism it is necessary to understand how he navigated the terrain of people-centred and state-centred Pan-Africanism. How did he serve as a head of state and as a founding member of the OAU while supporting a vision of people's freedom as manifest in the principles of Ujamaa? To understand this delicate manoeuvre it is worth making a short detour here to outline the 20th century renditions of Pan-Africanism in his lifetime.

Julius Nyerere matured as a youth during the capitalist depression and was initially educated in the cooperative traditions of the village community. As a youth he could not escape the ferment of the struggles against colonialism in all parts of the world and he studied in the United Kingdom after the fifth Pan-African Congress in 1945. Leaders such as W.E.B. Dubois, Kwame Nkrumah, George Padmore and numerous others were in the forefront of the call for self-determination and independence in this period. Gandhi, Nehru, Mao Tse Tsung and other leaders of a movement that was to be later called the Non-Aligned Movement (NAM) had been organising against imperialism and colonialism.

In Africa, the nationalist leaders such as Amilcar Cabral, Nelson Mandela, Kwame Nkrumah, Julius Nyerere and Jomo Kenyatta were influenced by the Non-Aligned Movement. African scholars usually refer to this period as the nationalist phase. The nationalist movement embraced the idea that independence was to be the basis for regeneration and reconstruction in Africa. Cheikh Anta Diop of Senegal and Frantz Fanon of Martinique were among those who transcended the preoccupation with governmental structures and sought to link the Pan-African project to the decolonisation of the mind. Fanon, as a psychiatrist, traced the mental illnesses associated with colonial rule in Algeria and linked the transformation of the health and sanity of the people to Pan-African liberation and African unity.

Cheikh Anta Diop reflected on the importance of African matriarchal traditions in what he called the Southern cradle of human transformations. Diop used the contributions of the Egyptian civilisations to write on the cultural and linguistic unity of Africa that was to be the basis of Pan-Africanism. Amilcar Cabral emphasised the role of national culture as a weapon of liberation.

The idea of Pan-African responsibility in the national liberation struggle was best articulated by both Nkrumah and Nyerere in the credo that the independence of one part of Africa would be meaningless until all of Africa was liberated from colonial rule and white minority domination such as apartheid. Nyerere was prepared to postpone the independence of Tanganyika and subordinate this objective to that of an independent East African federation, 'rather than take the risk of perpetuating the balkanisation of East Africa'. During this period of the armed struggles for independence, Nyerere along with Kenneth Kaunda and Tom Mboya were the driving forces behind the Pan-African Freedom Movement of East and Central Africa (PAFMECA).

In 1958, one year after the independence of Ghana, Nkrumah convened the first All African Peoples' Conference. It was at this meeting that members of the embryonic Civil Rights Movement of the United States came into contact with the mass movements that were fighting in Africa such as the Algerian and Kenyan struggles for independence. It was also at this meeting that Patrice Lumumba was introduced to the wider Pan-African community. The struggles over the independence of the Congo were to be a major test for the international Pan-African movement. The meeting to form PAFMECA was initiated by Nyerere, A.M. Babu, Tom Mboya and Kenneth Kaunda in Mwanza, Tanzania, in September 1958.

PAFMECA was in touch with the struggles in South Africa and, while fighting underground, Nelson Mandela made his way through Botswana and Zambia to Tanzania and then to Addis Ababa to address PAFMECA in 1962. After establishing the links to the struggles in southern Africa, PAFMECA changed its name to PAFMECSA (the Pan-African Freedom Movement for East, Central and Southern Africa) in order to coordinate support for liberation in all parts of eastern, central and southern Africa.

The full history of PAFMESCA and the hosting of all the liberation movements in Tanzania is still to be written. Such a history will bring to light the sacrifices of the Tanzanian peoples and the twists and turns involved in negotiating the building of an OAU Liberation Committee in a time when the OAU was dominated by people such as Mobutu Sese Seko, Hastings Banda and Félix Houphouët-Boigny, who were against liberation. Efforts to understand the twists and turns of the Lusaka Manifesto of 1969, the Mogadishu Declaration and the Mulungushi Club[1] based on decisions made by Nyerere will fail to grasp the depth of imperial machinations against African self-determination. The military overthrow of Milton Obote, attempts to militarily intervene in Tanzanian politics and the prolonged economic destabilisation of Tanzania were only some of the imperial efforts to derail the struggles for independence in Africa.

Tanzania and eastern Africa could not escape the ferment generated by the assassination of Patrice Lumumba, the US-supported mercenaries in eastern Congo along with the military support for Rhodesia and the apartheid infrastructure. Nyerere and Tanzania took the principled stand of breaking off diplomatic relations with Britain in 1965 after Ian Smith declared the unilateral declaration of independence in what was then Rhodesia. Freedom fighters from every liberation movement found a home in Tanzania: Frelimo of Mozambique; UNIP of Zambia; the Malawi Congress Party; ANC and PAC as well as the Unity Movement of South Africa; MPLA of Angola; SWAPO of Namibia; ZANU and ZAPU of Zimbabwe; and freedom fighters from as far afield as the Comoros. Nyerere could host these organisations because of the support from the Tanzanian peoples. It was this people-centred base for liberation that withstood all of the destabilisation plans of imperialism and apartheid. It was not by accident that Che Guevara used Tanzania as his 'base' (in that he entered and returned from the Congo via Tanzania) when he sought to join the liberation struggles in the Congo in 1965. It was unthinkable that Tanzania would enter into any form of imperial military alliance as the present government of Tanzania is doing by giving political cover for the US Africa Command.

Pan-Africanism and anti-dictatorial struggles

The independence of Mozambique, Angola, Zimbabwe, Namibia, and the coming to power of an African government in South Africa owe a great debt to the leadership of Nyerere and the sacrifices of the Tanzanian peoples. It was in this same spirit that Nyerere opposed Mobutism and supported the struggle for a new mode of politics in the Congo. His support for democracy and peace in the Congo was consistent with his life long opposition to African tyrants and those who seek to use ethnic, regional and religious divisions to weaken Africa.

Mwalimu Nyerere's support for the peoples of Uganda against the dictatorship of Idi Amin in Uganda (1971–79) was one of the most important lessons for those who are now seeking to build an African Union that is based on the security of the peoples and not the security of states. The military invasion of Uganda in 1978 defied the sterile position of the OAU: 'nonintervention in the internal affairs of other states'. Nyerere demonstrated that the killing of Africans in any part of Africa or any part of the world should be of concern to all human beings, especially African leaders. There were many who supported Idi Amin because he expelled the Asian traders from Uganda, but Nyerere demonstrated that oppression must be opposed even if the leader uses nationalist rhetoric to disguise the oppression. The opposition of Nyerere to Idi Amin and militarists must be continued. Micombero, the Burundi head of state, slaughtered hundreds of thousands in the country as genocidal politics took over eastern and central Africa. It is this tradition of genocidal politics and economics that calls for clarity in Africa so that there must be a line drawn against leaders of the African Union who manipulate the just struggles for land and justice in order to keep themselves in power. It is not in the interest of Africans to support a leader just because the western world is against that leader.

Global warming, desertification, the deterioration and loss of productivity in vast agricultural areas, the pollution of rivers and aquifers, the loss of biodiversity, the increase in natural catastrophes and the deforestation of rainforests require regional and continental intervention and it is unthinkable that leaders can find the resources to fight wars in other countries but cannot mobilise the resources for a vigorous fight for the lives of the African peoples. The objectives of promoting regional peace and security must be carried forward with renewed vigour. It is not in the interest of those who politicise ethnicity, regionalism and religion to teach the young in Africa about the heritage of Nyerere. Progressive Pan-Africanists have a lot to learn from a leader who remained studiously independent and ideologically self-reliant in the midst of the cold war.

Ujamaa, Ubuntu and African education

Ideological self-reliance meant that Nyerere was not dogmatic. Numerous writers and intellectuals attest to the free flow of ideas in Tanzania and the level of tolerance for differing points of views. It was this tolerance that enabled the free flow of ideas that characterised the intellectual climate of the Dar es Salaam school. Scholars such as Issa Shivji, Walter Rodney, Mahmood Mamdani, Michaela Von Freyhold, Yash Tandon, Clive Thomas, John Saul, Lionel Cliffe, Claude Ake, and countless others assisted in the transformation of the intellectual climate. Fennie Ginwala in journalism, Telford Georges in law along with countless others found a place in a society that was committed to socialism and self-reliance.

Ujamaa, the philosophy of Pan-African socialism, was announced as the official state policy of Tanzania in the Arusha Declaration of February 1967. This was the most ambitious effort to clarify the intersection between state-centred and people-centred Pan-Africanism. Ujamaa was original and drew from a body of thought that is to be found in all parts of Africa. Ujamaa embraced aspects of the Swahili concept of *utu* or common humanity (or Ubuntu as it is called in South Africa). This is based on the philosophy of forgiveness, reconciliation and willingness to share. It was this tradition that inspired the Truth and Reconciliation Commission in South Africa and generated a new climate of forgiveness. Humanity in Africa would still be in the midst of a more violent war if the leaders of South Africa (such as Nelson Mandela and Desmond Tutu) had decided to take revenge on those apartheid leaders who killed two million and wreaked over $80 billion worth of destruction in the region of southern Africa. This experience of forgiveness and the new politics of truth and reconciliation warn us that the present war against terror that is being waged by the government of the USA is misguided and has the potential to unleash massive insecurity and millions of deaths in the world. It is in the traditions of peace, reparations and justice that this celebration of the life of Nyerere must be used as an opportunity to oppose the militarisation of the planet and the manipulation of religion and spiritual relations.

Nyerere provided moral leadership in a continent where many leaders thought of filling their pockets and bank accounts instead of serving their people. Though he was a Christian he wore a *kofia* as a symbolic identification with the Islamic followers in his society. Nyerere as a people-centred Pan-Africanist was opposed to all forms of religious intolerance. It would never be in his vocabulary to suggest that there were some societies that are based on evil. Even when it was clear that apartheid terror was destroying the lives of the peoples of southern Africa, Nyerere was not fighting the whites of South Africa; he was opposed to the ideas and practices of apartheid and capitalism.

Mwalimu Nyerere was a revolutionary leader of the 20th century who opposed the capitalists with fervour. His opposition to the World Bank and the International Monetary Fund (IMF) was one of the epic struggles against global capitalism in the last century. The idea of ujamaa villages and a form of social collectivism that dug deep into the African past is one that will inspire millions for this millennium. Physicists and other scientists who are now recognising the limitations of crude materialism are turning to the ideas of leaders such as Nyerere to warn humanity to retreat from the crude and mechanistic ideas of the domination over nature that has brought about ecological disaster. Mwalimu struggled to maintain the harmony between humans and their environment. Throughout his political career he battled against the expropriation of poor peasants from the land. He wanted all of the people to own the land and up to his last days he was opposed to the privatisation of land and the land policies of the IMF. Many apologists for local and international capitalism have suggested that Ujamaa was a failure but these are the same forces who lauded apartheid as an economic success. One cannot be successful economically when the majority of the population is without food, clothing, shelter and healthcare. The policies of Ujamaa enabled Tanzania to enjoy one of the highest literacy rates in the world.

It is also important to grasp the limits of Nyerere as a leader of a neocolonial state that was isolated by international capitalism. Abdul Rahman Babu has collaborated with Amrit Wilson (1989) to write on *US Foreign Policy and Revolution: the Creation of Tanzania*. Here Babu contributed to our understanding of US machinations against self-determination in Tanzania after the Zanzibar Revolution in 1964. We must also use this opportunity to commemorate leaders such as Nyerere in order to be self-critical;

we must be open to a reassessment of experiences during the period of Nyerere's leadership. These experiences must be discussed so that contemporary efforts toward regional unity, such as the eastern African economic community, can learn from the strengths and weaknesses of previous agreements and the political leaders who wrought them.

Although I say this, I am not one who believed that the Ujamaa project was an error. I believe that the Ujamaa project was valid and its validity will be tested in another period when the struggles for peace and reparations move from opposition to structural transformation of the old colonial economic realities. Any shortcomings in the union between Tanganyika and Zanzibar must be rectified so that they do not fester and become a basis for eroding the stability of Tanzania. One other controversial decision of Nyerere was his support for the breakaway state of Biafra 1967–70. Along with all the praise of Nyerere, it should be remembered that he was also human and was not a 'saint' in the course of his long political career. It is important to honour his memory by highlighting his positive contributions to emancipatory politics in Africa.

It is also important for all of us to understand that Nyerere was far in advance of his peers in recognising many of the strengths of the African village community, including the knowledge system. He recognised that there was an alternative knowledge system that was embedded in the languages and cultures of the African peoples. Those who are studying fractal mathematics are now turning to African fractals in order to grasp the full implications of chaos and complexity.

The decision to make Kiswahili the language of business, commerce and government in Tanzania ensured that the peoples of the country were drawn into the decision-making process. Education for self-reliance fired up the imagination of the poor in Tanzania and the stability of Tanzania is in large part due to the cohesion and unity fostered by the language policies of Nyerere as well as the positive steps during the period of education for self-reliance. It is imperative that the Tanzanian government deepens the study of African ideas and cultures in order to make a significant contribution to the 21st century world. The language policy of Tanzania is an important platform from which genuine bilingual traditions can develop so that students in schools and universities are not alienated in their own country. The unfinished tasks of making the national language a language of higher education will ensure the rapid social and economic transformation of Tanzania.

At the same time we want to remember the positive ideals of Ujamaa and collective solidarity that became a tradition. The concept of *ndugu* (a gender neutral concept signifying brotherhood and sisterhood) was a new concept of inclusion and citizenship that was opposed to all forms of xenophobia in Africa. The Third World Conference against Racism (held in Durban in September 2001) has made the need for truth and reparations clearer. This conference and the subsequent acknowledgment that colonialism and slavery were crimes against humanity should be popularised so that the world can retreat from the celebration of slavery and genocide as progress. The need to document and expose the crimes of Europe and the USA in Africa is as urgent as the fight against warfare and genocidal violence in Africa

Reparations and the Pan-African world

The demand to repair the planet earth at the UN summit on climate change at Copenhagen in December 2009 brought to the forefront a new conception of reparations. It was in this international meeting that the present leaders of the African Union exposed their alliance with the leaders of western mining and oil companies against the interests of the poor. Characteristically, it was the South African and Ethiopian leadership that exposed this gross betrayal. Forced to choose between environmental justice for the people and the international corporations, the representatives of the African Union and the South African leadership made their choice with international capital.

The Pan-African Climate Justice Alliance is emerging as a new continental coalition of people-centred Pan-Africanists who are coming together in the African continent to organise against the destruction of the natural environment. Similarly, it was in South Africa where another people-oriented organisation, the Treatment Action Campaign, led the fight against President Mbeki and the international pharmaceutical industry. Whether the Pan African Climate Justice Alliance survives as a people-centred Pan-African formation will depend on the extent to which this organisation builds links with the grassroots and becomes self reliant at the intellectual and organisational level.

It is now clearer in the struggles for health and a clean environment that the present governments and leaders in Africa constitute an obstacle to Pan-African liberation and emancipation. Philosophically, a new cadre of intellectuals has been interrogating the old state-centred philosophy of Pan-Africanism. At the end of the 20th century, Phillippe Wamba's book on *Kinship* moved the level of discussion from the politics of movements to the lived experiences of Africans at home and abroad. In this way, Phillippe Wamba was able to represent Pan-Africanism at the levels both of theoretical and intellectual discourses and the day-to-day life of African peoples. Wamba was using an idea of kinship that goes beyond traditional biological kinship to a cultural concept of kinship which echoed Cheikh Anta Diop's view of *The Cultural Unity of Black Africa*. It is not by accident that Wamba gained his insights while he was a youth in Tanzania.

Wamba cited the symbolically relevant Baldwin quote: a gulf of 'three hundred years' of alienation was too 'vast to be conquered in an evening's goodwill'. What he successfully did in drawing from the culture of emancipation – manifest in the work of Fela Ransome Kuti, Paul Robeson, Hugh Masakela, John Coltrane, Aretha Franklin, Tupac Shakur, Bob Marley and countless other cultural leaders – was to show that people-centred Pan-Africanism transcended geography and territories. Pan-African emancipation was an active search through the complexity of encounter on both sides of the Atlantic. Pan-Africanism, therefore, as Wamba's own journey testifies, can only be understood via its multifaceted dimensions.

It was Bob Marley who, through both the medium and the message, called for a conception of African unity and human freedom which was linked to the emancipation from mental slavery. Bob Marley wanted to transcend racial divisions, with a universal message of African unity, love, peace and human emancipation. The challenge for Pan-Africanism in the 21st century is to take the conception of emancipation beyond the material plane to grasp the limits of the human potential imposed by the eugenic civilisation of the contemporary period.

Navigating the terrain of Pan-Africanism today

Julius Nyerere did not confine his contribution to the African continent. As the chairperson of the South Commission after 1985 he worked hard to build linkages between the peoples and governments of the South. This work was a continuation of his earlier efforts to break the hegemony of western financial institutions. Nyerere worked very closely with Fidel Castro and Michael Manley in calling for a New International Economic Order. This call is now being carried forward in the context of the Bolivarian Alternative for Latin America and the Caribbean.

Nyerere was very aware that the majority of the citizens of Latin America were black and indigenous peoples. He had studied world history so understood the deliberate policies to whiten Latin America and that in some countries such as Argentina and Paraguay, the racist policies and violence against Africans and indigenous peoples reached genocidal proportions. For this reason the African population in these countries is very small, but throughout Latin America there are millions of Africans, with Brazil counting over 80 million Africans. Significant populations of African peoples are to be found in Brazil, Panama, Colombia, Ecuador, Peru, Venezuela, Honduras, Cuba, the Dominican Republic, Puerto Rica, Costa Rica, Nicaragua and Mexico. Black populations range in size from less than 1 per cent to as high as 30 per cent in Colombia and 46 per cent in Brazil. They are majorities in some Spanish-speaking Caribbean nations: Cuba and the Dominican Republic. In 1996 the Inter American Development Bank estimated that there were over 150 million Africans in the region of Central and South America, 'about a third of the region's population, are descendants of African slaves. Other estimates are lower because many people of mixed race do not define themselves as Black.'

The democratic openings in Latin America in the past decade have brought the question of people-to-people relations between the Americas and Africa to the centre of international politics. With the election of Hugo Chavez in Venezuela and Evo Morales in Bolivia, the issues of race and racism have re-emerged as fundamental questions in the liberation struggles of Latin America. Pan-Africanists in the 21st century are linking with the new struggles for liberation in Latin America to reassert the principles of liberation and emancipation of peoples struggling everywhere. Hugo Chavez attests to the lessons that he learnt form Nyerere. It is therefore not by accident that the Bank of the South (a new financial institution that is organised to break the power of the IMF and World Bank) seeks to build on Nyerere's work as head of the South Commission.

From as early as 1961 Nyerere held forth on the barbarism of capitalism, reminded his audience of the economic underpinnings of the scramble for Africa and the need for a socialist option to escape this form of domination. In outlining the differing forms of partition and division since the 1885 Berlin conference, Nyerere, in a speech given to the World Assembly of Youth, asserted his belief that 'no underdeveloped country can afford to be anything but socialist'. This speech reflected his confidence in the youth. The quotation was within a context where Nyerere was not only discussing the economic way forward but also stressing that the path of socialism is impossible outside of a united Africa. The ideas of Ujamaa were later articulated as an antidote to the barbarism that James wrote about. C.L.R. James lauded Ujamaa and called it one of the true roads to freedom. Nyerere has written volumes on the issue of freedom and unity and stands in the ranks of those intellectuals who tackled the issue of barbarism not only in theory but also in practice.

Pan-African questions today

By the end of the 20th century African women had emerged with a new definition of Pan-Africanism that emphasised the humanity of Africans and not simply the independence of states. Micere Mugo, the Kenyan freedom fighter, stated clearly that African women represented the essence, if not the substance, of Pan-Africanism over the centuries. As a man, Nyerere's agricultural and economic policies were male centred. African women are demanding health and investments in the provision of food, clothing, shelter, environmental justice and safety. These women are opposing all forms of gender discrimination and gendered oppression. The reality for the 21st century of biotechnology, eugenics, patenting life forms and new diseases forced Pan-Africanists to understand questions of health and wellness as core principles of Pan-African freedom and African dignity. In the process, there is a clearer need for an emancipatory framework that interrogates issues of class, gender and sexuality. These forces are at the forefront of opposing the frightening homophobic policies that are being promoted in a number of African societies.

Nyerere distinguished himself from those leaders in Africa who opposed colonialism, but simply wanted an Africanisation of the state. The death of millions of Africans every day requires radical interventions and one of the medium-term tasks of the present Pan-African liberation is to build an international coalition while linking to the day-to-day struggles for peace and reconstruction.

The concern with the survival of Africans as human beings, with the natural environment and the relations between humans and nature has been vividly brought to the forefront for the citizens of the world, given the destructive capabilities of capitalism. Julius Nyerere was never shy in spelling out the impact of this destruction in his time and was uncompromising in his belief that the national liberation process must simultaneously be a struggle for internationalism and a struggle against imperialism. Nyerere was never seduced by the technology of capitalism because he was aware of the destruction that was unleashed in his time by the massive world war and the genocide that was the hallmark of civilisation. In the present period the technological imperative to militarism has not abated, but the thrust is to move the wars and genocide to parts of the world where there are Africans and other peoples of colour.

How can humanity develop the kind of collective leadership that is based on the values of social collectivism to emancipate human beings all over the world? Nyerere was clear that this emancipation required a revolution. At the time of the Arusha Declaration he said,

We have been exploited a great deal,
We have been oppressed a great deal,
Now is the time for a revolution.

This call for revolution is still meaningful and the challenge of those in the forefront of liberation is to navigate the terrain of states to build a new international movement for human survival. People-centred Pan-Africanism is critical in the fight for human survival.

Mwalimu Nyerere was a humble person who was incorruptible in a world of corruption. He continues to be an inspiration to revolutionaries and his internationalism will be a guide to the work to free humans who want to fight against racism, militarism, exploitation and destruction of the environment.

Note

1. The Lusaka Manifesto was adopted by the leaders of the states of southern Africa (except Malawi). This manifesto put forward the position that the heads of state would dissuade the liberation movements from continuing the armed struggle if the Portuguese and South African regimes accepted the principles of independence and majority rule and agreed to start the process of negotiations to that end. This position was adopted by the leaders of the OAU.

The Mogadishu Declaration of 1971 nullified the Lusaka Manifesto. The declaration argued that since the Portuguese colonialists and the apartheid regime had not responded positively, frustrating the hopes of the OAU, there was no alternative but to continue to support the armed struggle.

The Mulungushi Club was the precursor of the Frontline States. Before the independence of Mozambique and Angola in 1975, Tanzania was virtually isolated as a society supporting self-determination. In an effort to mobilise leaders to support liberation the Mulungushi Club (named after the place of its first meeting, Mulungushi, Zambia) involved the heads of state of Tanzania, Uganda, Zambia and Zaire. This short-lived grouping began to split apart when Milton Obote was overthrown in Uganda in January 1971. Mobutu was a member of this club but the more robust formation called the Frontline States ended the solution of Tanzania after the independence of Mozambique and Angola. The leaders of the liberation movements recognised by the OAU were invited to the meetings of the club.

Bibliography

Amadiume, Ifi (1998) *Reinventing Africa: Matriarchy, Religion and Culture*, London, Zed Books

Babu, Abdul Rahman and Wilson, Amrit (1989) *US Foreign Policy and Revolution: the Creation of Tanzania*, London, Pluto Press

Babu, A.M. (2002) *The Future that Works*, Lawrenceville, NJ, Africa World Press

Diop, Cheikh Anta (1989) *The Cultural Unity of Black Africa: The Domains of Matriarchy and Patriarchy*, London, Karnak House, 'Foreward' and 'Introduction'

Eglash, Ron (1999) *African Fractals: Modern Computing and Indigenous Design*, Piscataway, NJ, Rutgers University Press

Fanon, Franz (1965) *The Wretched of the Earth,* Grove Pess, New York

Nyerere, J. (1974) *Freedom and Development, Uhuru Na Maendeleo,* Dar es Salaam, Oxford University Press

Mugo, Micere (2002) 'Re-envisioning Pan-Africanism: what is the role of gender, youth and the masses?' in Mandaza, Ibbo and Nabudere, Dan (eds) *Pan-Africanism and Integration in Africa,* Harare, SAPES Books

Nyerere, J. (1977) *Ujamaa – Essays on Socialism,* London, Oxford University Press

Nyerere, J. (1979) *Crusade for Liberation,* Dar es Salaam, Oxford University Press

Rodney, Walter (1975) 'Towards the sixth Pan-African Congress: aspects of the international class struggle in *Africa, the Caribbean and America',* in Horace Campbell (ed) *Pan-Africanism: Struggle Against Neo-colonialism and Imperialism – Documents of the Sixth Pan-African Congress,* Toronto, Afro-Carib Publications

Rodney, Walter (1990) *Walter Rodney Speaks: the Making of an African Intellectual,* Lawrenceville, NJ, Africa World Press

Thompson, V.B. (1969) *Africa and Unity: The Evolution of Pan-Africanism,* London, Longmans

Wamba, Philippe (1999) *Kinship: A Family's Journey in Africa and America,* New York, NY, Dutton

Nyerere, the Organisation of African Unity and liberation

Mohamed Sahnoun

On 24 May 1963, the Addis Ababa Conference of Independent African States met for the first time under the chairmanship of its host, Emperor Haille Selassie of Ethiopia. I attended as a member of the Algerian delegation led by President Ben Bella who, together with other heads of state from that first generation of nationalists such as Presidents Nkrumah, Nasser, Sékou Touré and, of course, Julius Nyerere, adopted the Charter of the Organisation of African Unity (OAU).

This was my first contact with President Nyerere, who, at this same meeting, led his colleagues to create a subsidiary organ of the OAU, the OAU Liberation Committee, which, at his invitation, set up its headquarters in Dar es Salaam. To say that President Nyerere was committed to – and forward looking in – the struggle for liberation in Africa even at that early stage is an understatement.

The following year, at the Cairo OAU summit, the heads of state elected Diallo Telli of Guinea to be the first secretary general of the OAU and myself as one of the two deputy secretaries general. My own mandate covered the area of political affairs, with special responsibility for the Liberation Committee. As such, I was for the next ten years a regular visitor to Dar es Salaam, home and rear-base to refugees and liberation movements from all over Africa.

The Liberation Committee, working under the guidance of a governing board of OAU member states, periodically elected by the heads of state and in close collaboration with the government of Tanzania and its designated officials and structures, provided funding, logistical support, training and publicity to all liberation movements officially recognised by the OAU. The committee also organised their presence and campaigns on the diplomatic front through conferences, visits, press campaigns and radio broadcasts.

In this way, I was in regular and direct contact with President Nyerere, who gave to every issue, no matter how secondary, his complete and consistent attention. His lucidity and his strategic skills were remarkable at all levels, as was his courage, bearing in mind that his own country was newly independent (1961) and that its state institutions were also at their formative stage.

Furthermore, the international context at that time was one of intense East–West rivalry and relentless cold war pressure. President Nyerere not only gave refuge and support to diverse liberation movements but also managed to navigate through the choppy seas of big power priorities and conflicts with consummate mastery. In this way, he and other African leaders were able to build a broad front of solidarity and support, material and diplomatic, from Africa, Asia, the Non-Aligned Movement, the Nordic countries and, of course, both China and the USSR.

This long period of collaboration with the president helped me to appreciate, indeed, to deepen, my own understanding of his complete and unfailing commitment to unity and solidarity for the benefit of the remaining parts of Africa still under colonial and racist domination. Unity and liberation were the two main tasks the OAU had set itself and President Nyerere served both these principles with his powerful intellectual and political skills.

For example, the Francophone states of Africa, then grouped within the French-led organisation OCAM, were initially not too keen on the formation of a continent-wide organisation such as the OAU. However, the arguments presented by the Tanzanian president were undeniable and these states could not but join the rest of the continent, much to the disapproval of France.

Again, when the question of the seat for the headquarters for the OAU Secretariat came up for discussion, President Nkrumah, at the suggestion of the francophone states, proposed Bangui, capital of the Central African Republic, on the grounds that Bangui was at the geographical centre of the entire African continent. President Nyerere, however, persuaded his colleagues to choose Addis Ababa on the grounds that it was the capital of the continent's oldest independent state.

As President Nyerere explained many times, it was because of the OAU that Africa as a whole had a presence and a voice in a world dominated by superpowers and former empires, where it could design its own priorities and solutions. The OAU was the only continental organisation in the post-colonial Third World; neither Asia nor Latin America had such an institution and this was the reason why Africa had a say in international matters, provided it used its unity as its strength.

When conflicts occurred, as they inevitably did at the OAU and in the area of liberation politics, Nyerere, as the *mwalimu* (teacher) that he was, used his gifts of analysis and reasoning to reach the right resolutions. For example, the assassination of Eduardo Mondlane, the founder of Frelimo, caused a serious leadership crisis for the Mozambican struggle. The Angolan freedom fighters also had their problems as did the leaders of SWAPO. Mwalimu was tireless in his efforts in the resolution of these difficulties, making sure that the real objectives were always kept in sight.

When necessary, he was also fearless in standing his own ground in the face of people like Ian Smith of Rhodesia and his unilateral declaration of independence. This was an illegal act and the British had the responsibility of bringing Smith to order, declared Nyerere, and if they did not, his country would end diplomatic relations with the UK. When the British did not act, this is exactly what happened in 1965.

President Nyerere worked closely with President Kaunda of Zambia, also a border state and rear-base to the ANC, MPLA and SWAPO, and these two statesmen, with their evident simplicity, their sense of humour and their sophisticated use of the English language, dominated the OAU summits over the years as their other comrades (Ben Bella, Nkrumah, Nasser) left the stage.

As the solidarity front strengthened over time, some memorable events took place:

- President Kaunda's mission to the Nordic countries on behalf of the OAU resulted in the Oslo Conference Against Apartheid in 1972, which was a major meeting of support and made a strong impact on European civic society.

- At the invitation of the OAU, I accompanied the deputy director general of UNESCO, Mokhtar M'Bow of Senegal, on his visits to Zambia and Tanzania in 1972 to meet the liberation movements and to see the work and structures of support provided by the host countries. At the end of the visits we had a memorable meeting with President Nyerere. On his return to Paris, M'Bow presented his report to UNESCO's general conference, which adopted his recommendation that the representatives of all liberation movements recognised by the OAU be invited to participate at UNESCO with observer status. This groundbreaking resolution was subsequently adopted by the entire UN system and led to the banning of racist South Africa from international activity and to its pariah status within the international community.

- In 1973, the Cairo OAU summit adopted a major resolution proposed by President Nyerere on the question of border conflicts that had started to erupt between the newly independent states trying to live within borders arbitrarily drawn in colonial times. (There had been serious confrontations between Niger and Dahomey – now Benin – and between Ghana and Ivory Coast.) The president argued for – and succeeded in getting adopted – the historic resolution on the inviolability and permanence of borders inherited from the colonial period on the grounds that peace and security issues were more important in independent Africa than trying to redraw borders.

- The Afro-Asian Solidarity Conference in Arusha was another landmark gathering of support for the anti-apartheid and liberation cause from Asia, China, the USSR and the entire Soviet bloc. As expected, there was some early friction between the Chinese and USSR delegations, both representing countries very active in their support for the liberation struggle. Once more, Mwalimu, greatly respected by both these powers, was able to resolve the problems and the meeting went ahead, with strong participation from ASEAN.

My own mandate at the OAU came to an end in 1974, a year that brought an important success for the liberation struggle: the April revolution in Lisbon led by young officers of the Portuguese army. The downfall of the Salazar regime in Lisbon was a consequence of its doomed effort, on behalf of the NATO states, to stem the freedom tide in southern Africa. The Portuguese soldiers saw the futility of this endeavour and returned home to liberate their own land from 40 years of fascism and begin the process of freeing their African colonies from 500 years of exploitation and severe underdevelopment.

It is fair to say that from its inception, the OAU and its Liberation Committee in Dar es Salaam were indelibly marked by Nyerere's commitment and leadership, by his realistic and inclusive strategies, his capacity to inspire and galvanise people from very different backgrounds and, of course, by his serene confidence, his eloquence and his unfailing good humour.

It was a unique privilege to have worked with such a leader.

Nyerere and the Commonwealth

Chief Emeka Anyaoku talks to Annar Cassam

The sun set over the British empire in the aftermath of World War II and simultaneously, with the independence of India in 1948, there was born a new multinational institution: the Commonwealth of Nations. The new republic of India became its first non-white member in 1949, joining the older ex-dominions of Canada, Australia, New Zealand and South Africa.

Ghana, the first independent country from Africa, joined in 1957 and the decade of the 1960s began with a memorable episode in international diplomacy initiated by Julius Nyerere, the leader of the soon-to-be-independent Tanganyika in 1961. The stage was the annual Commonwealth prime ministers' meeting in London in March 1961. On the eve of this gathering, Nyerere (whose own country's Uhuru date was already set for December 1961) wrote a letter to the *Observer* and the *Manchester Guardian* which seriously rattled the British establishment.

The letter also, and above all, shook the South African government for it questioned the presence of a racist regime in an international institution based on the principles of mutual respect and equality among all nations, new and old. The issue under discussion at that meeting concerned South Africa's request to remain in the Commonwealth as it changed its status from dominion to republic. How could Africa join an organisation which had as its member a state which applied apartheid and white supremacy as its official policy, asked Nyerere. In a well-argued letter, he explained that his country would decline to seek membership in such a situation, for 'to vote South Africa in is to vote us out'. Furthermore, Tanganyika's example could well be followed by other African, Asian and Caribbean countries soon to gain independence from the UK.

The case was unanswerable and Nyerere was seconded by the then prime minister of Canada, John Diefenbaker, who took on the task of 'persuading' his South African counterpart (Henrik Verwoerd) to withdraw from the Commonwealth rather than face being expelled from it. The South Africans left the meeting forthwith, Mwalimu remained and a year later, Tanganyika was welcomed as a full member.

This event was recalled by the distinguished Nigerian diplomat, Emeka Anyaoku, who spent 34 years at the Commonwealth Secretariat and who became its secretary general from 1990 to 2000. As he explained, he had the privilege of observing, aiding and accompanying President Nyerere in his many interventions and initiatives on behalf of Africa and the Third World in general and on behalf of the liberation struggle of South and southern Africa in particular. In many of these instances, the president came into serious conflict with the British government of the day, for the Commonwealth connection did not turn out to be the cosy network they had perhaps once imagined.

A most difficult chapter opened in 1965 when Ian Smith, head of the white settlers in control of the British colony of Rhodesia, declared himself and the colony 'independent' of British rule under a unilateral declaration of independence (UDI). The matter was discussed at the Organisation of African Unity (OAU) summit that year and President Nyerere and his colleagues demanded in a resolution that the British government take responsibility for this illegal act of usurpation on the part of Smith, failing which OAU member states would end diplomatic relations with the UK.

Mwalimu argued that the British should follow the example of General de Gaulle, who had had to face a similar challenge from some French settlers in Algeria, whose attempt to act unilaterally had been rejected forcefully by the general. The Labour government of Harold Wilson refused to force Smith to return to legality and in December 1965, Tanzania and Ghana ended all diplomatic contacts with the UK.

As Chief Anyaoku points out, the matter did not rest there. Mwalimu was consistent in his relentless opposition to racist politics no matter where these were manifest. In this way, he mobilised and inspired many other Commonwealth citizens. One such was the first secretary general of the Commonwealth, the Canadian Arnold Smith, appointed in 1965. In 1966, at the meeting of the Commonwealth law ministers, held in London, Arnold Smith solved the dilemma of the break in relations between the UK administration and the African states mentioned above in an innovative manner. He invited and encouraged these delegations to come to London because he took the position that the Commonwealth was an international organisation whose activities were not subject to the policies of the host government. He cited the presence of Cuba at the UN in New York as an example. The law ministers in question duly attended the meeting at Marlborough House, London.

In July of the same year, these countries also attended the heads of state and government meeting in London where, once more, Nyerere led the charge to get the British to act on Ian Smith in Rhodesia. The African group demanded action in the form of sanctions against Rhodesia, but the British prime minister merely proposed talks with the rebel regime. As a result, the Africans proposed and the summit adopted the famous resolution on NIBMAR (No Independence Before Majority African Rule), which cornered the British, if not the Rhodesian rebels, in a significant manner.

By the time of the 1971 Commonwealth summit, held in Singapore, another conflict had arisen between Nyerere and the British government, now led by Prime Minister Edward Heath. The British gave notice of their decision to revive the Simonstown Agreement with South Africa for the sale of British arms to that country. Mwalimu protested that these arms were destined to be used against the black population of South Africa and as such the agreement was indefensible. The British rejected this argument based on the legalistic position of the duty of states to respect treaty obligations. Matters came to a head at Singapore when Mwalimu, supported by President Kaunda of Zambia and President Obote of Uganda, strongly challenged Prime Minister Heath over the Simonstown Agreement. In the end, the British bowed to pressure from Africa and the rest of the Commonwealth, but a heavy price was paid at the summit by Uganda, whose president was deposed in a coup d'état while attending the meeting and whose population subsequently suffered for years under the bloody and demented reign of Idi Amin.

These summits were not always so confrontational, as Chief Anyaoku points out. Mwalimu was not always on the warpath in these meetings. His preferred method was a mixture of intellectual argument and gentle humour as at the 1975 summit in Jamaica. During the discussion on the liberation struggle in Africa, President Kaunda had given an emotional statement praising the solidarity and concrete help given to the liberation movements by China and the USSR. Whereupon Prime Minister Lee Kwan Yew of Singapore chided him for having 'let the cat out of the bag' by revealing an open secret. Mwalimu immediately diffused the situation with a memorable and spontaneous aphorism, namely that 'when the mice are out, we must let out the cat!'

The years 1974–75 brought momentous changes for the liberation struggle in Africa with the collapse of the Salazar regime in Lisbon, the liberation of Mozambique by Frelimo and the attempted South African invasion of Angola, which was thwarted by Cuban military assistance to the besieged MPLA government in Luanda. These events destabilised the cold war boundary-lines in Africa which the West had taken for granted and which the USA especially could not abandon, caught as the Americans were in an ideological time-warp of their own making, in spite of their defeat in Vietnam in 1975. Henry Kissinger's visit to Dar es Salaam in 1977 to meet Nyerere, chairman of the Frontline States, was a belated and futile exercise in shuttle diplomacy; times had changed and so had the realities on the ground.

By 1979, the Commonwealth too had changed and into this changed world stepped the next British prime minister, Margaret Thatcher, to face a cast of experienced old-timers such as Nyerere, Kaunda, Ian Smith and the Queen, the perennial symbolic head of the Commonwealth. The organisation's secretary general was now the former attorney general of Guyana, Shridath 'Sonny' Ramphal, and his deputy was Emeka Anyaoku, the living institutional memory of the organisation.

The liberation struggle in southern Africa had also been transformed by the formation of the Frontline States (FLS – Tanzania, Zambia, Mozambique, Botswana and Angola) under the chairmanship of President Nyerere. The next chapter in the

FLS strategy centred on the liberation of Rhodesia from the illegal grip of Ian Smith, who had never been challenged by the British crown and who had by now made the place into a 'republic'. In 1979, under a so-called 'internal settlement', Smith appointed the first black prime minister, Bishop Abel Muzorewa, and began to negotiate with the new British government for formal recognition.

At President Kaunda's invitation, the venue of the 1979 Commonwealth summit was Lusaka and the date was set for August. In May of that year, it became known that Mrs Thatcher was preparing to recognise the Muzorewa government in spite of the fact that the British had ended formal diplomatic ties with Smith some years previously. In July, the rightwing prime minister of New Zealand, Robert Muldoon, came to London to lunch with Mrs Thatcher, following which he gave a press conference to explain to the media how very concerned he and the British prime minster were, about the level of safety and security arrangements for the Queen during her stay in Lusaka. Within hours, Buckingham Palace reacted with a statement to the effect that 'it remained the firm intention of Her Majesty to attend the Lusaka Commonwealth Summit'.

As can be imagined, at Lusaka the African heads of state argued very forcefully against any links with the Muzorewa regime and for direct talks between the British authorities and the leaders of the liberation movements, such as Joshua Nkomo, Josiah Tongogara and Robert Mugabe. Mrs Thatcher was isolated and outclassed by all her Commonwealth colleagues from around the globe, including New Zealand and Australia. The Queen, exceptionally, extended her stay in Lusaka beyond the first day's formal opening and the summit in its entirety passed a resolution which led to the organisation of the Lancaster House talks, the temporary return of Rhodesia to colonial status under the British and the eventual agreement to prepare for majority rule and independence for Zimbabwe.

Mwalimu attended his last Commonwealth summit as president of Tanzania in 1985 in the Bahamas and once more had to ensure, together with President Kaunda, that the organisation's efforts over South Africa were not diluted by British interests. The Bahamas summit had decided to send an Eminent Persons Group (the EPG) to South Africa to meet the leadership there to ascertain the seriousness of their declarations regarding political change in that country.

After the summit ended and before the EPG set out, the British press announced that the EPG would be led by Mrs Thatcher's foreign secretary, Sir Geoffrey Howe. The reactions from Dar es Salaam and Lusaka were immediate and unequivocal: the two presidents rejected the very idea of the EPG if led by the British. Chief Emeka Anyaoku flew to meet Mwalimu and subsequently to see President Kaunda to reassure them that the EPG would be led not by the British but by two co-chairmen: General Olesegun Obasanjo of Nigeria and Malcolm Fraser of Australia.

Finally, former Secretary General Anyaoku recounts with pride that it was at the Kuala Lumpur summit of 1989 that the Commonwealth leaders took the initiative of establishing the South Commission and the South Centre and invited Mwalimu Nyerere to be the chairman.

This was a fitting and lasting tribute to a champion of South–South cooperation and an advocate of the South in global affairs. Throughout his long and creative association with the many international forums he attended, he brilliantly practised what he believed – the common humanity and equality of all. At the Commonwealth, he led by example and so shaped the history of the institution and the very meaning of international solidarity.

Chief Emeka Anyaoku was interviewed by Annar Cassam in London in September 2009.

President Nyerere talks to *El País* (1991)

Interviewed by Ana Camacho

It has been six years since Julius Nyerere retired from the political scene in Tanzania, a country he led for 30 years, starting with the struggle for independence. A rare example in Africa, he retired of his own volition without being forced out by a military coup or a revolution.

'The Tanzanians began wondering anxiously about what would happen when Mwalimu went', Julius Nyerere explained to us at *El País* during his visit to Madrid. 'In such a case, it was no use saying, "Wait until I die in order to find out!"', he joked. 'And so I handed the reins to my successors and said, "Let us take the risk together".'

A graduate of Edinburgh University and translator of Shakespeare into Kiswahili, the national language, he knew how to avoid the risks of tribalism by forging a nation state whose final form culminated in the Union of Tanganyika and Zanzibar in 1964. A devout Roman Catholic, his dream was Ujamaa, a form of socialism which rejects western concepts of capitalism and Marxism, but has, at its core, a belief in the importance of the agrarian society (Tanzania, like the rest of sub-Saharan Africa, is overwhelmingly a peasant society) and of family solidarity.

For the last two years, he has dedicated himself to travelling the globe in order to speak of the conclusions of the South Commission, which he established in 1987.

Camacho: Do you think that the current developments in eastern Europe [after the fall of the Berlin Wall and the end of the Soviet–Russian domination of that part of Europe] will lead to a reduction in western aid to the countries of the South ?

Nyerere: There is a real feeling that we are going to be forgotten by the so-called First World. We need to have a rethink here, and in the South Commission report we say that the development of our own countries is above all our own responsibility. If the countries of the South want development, they will have to initiate it themselves by making clear political choices.

Accordingly, our first recommendation is that if African countries want to develop in freedom, they must put their own people, their own money and their own resources to maximum use. Another problem is that when our countries talk of external cooperation partnerships, they only think of the North. They never consider the possibility of South–South cooperation, say between southern Africa and Latin America. Finally, in order to attract foreign investment to the South, it is first of all vital for local people themselves to invest in their own countries instead of sending their capital abroad.

Camacho: To what point can democracy be of help in African countries in their quest for development?

Nyerere: Democracy can help to motivate our people when they are asked to tighten their belts so that they do not feel they are doing this for the benefit of the dictator of the day. But one should not confuse the sense of freedom with the issue of basic needs arising from hunger, the lack of schools, the insufficiency of transportation and electricity networks. And to believe that, with the advent of multiparty politics, all causes of economic distress will vanish overnight can create a dangerous delusion and lead to military *coups d'état*.

Camacho: The disorder and chaos facing eastern Europe appear to have sounded the death-knell of socialism and the triumph of capitalism…

Nyerere: Yes, now we see the birth of a new god, one called capitalism, which supposedly has all the answers. But to conclude that socialism has failed because of what has happened in the Soviet Union is equivalent to saying Christianity has failed because 2,000 years after Jesus Christ urged us to 'turn the other cheek ' or to 'love your enemy as you love yourself', these recommendations have yet to be complied with.

Moreover, I have never considered the Soviets to be true

socialists, exactly as they too do not believe that I am an authentic socialist. In Tanzania, we said this very clearly in the Arusha Declaration in 1967: there is no socialism without freedom. And of course, when I visited the USSR in 1969, I saw clearly that Soviet citizens were not free.

Camacho: You will no doubt admit that you have yourself not succeeded in fulfilling your own socialist project...

Nyerere: Yes, there have been mistakes, but in application; the idea still remains valid and if I had to start again, I would do the same things. What matters is that socialism be based on one's attitude; it cannot be imposed by force.

Socialism, as an idea of a just society, cannot die. I know that in these times, one is not supposed to say such things. But I belong to a dying breed which resists reneging on its ideals!

Some would say that it is no use believing in such things, but does it make more sense to believe in a society based on General Motors? I reject this. At present, we are living a moment of deception. But the conditions being created on the ground by this euphoria over capitalism give me reason to believe that in about ten years or so, the ideal of socialism will return – and more forcefully than before.

Originally published in El País, *Madrid, 16 November 1991. English translation by Annar Cassam.*

Annar Cassam comments on Nyerere's *El País* interview

Our first recommendation (in the Report of the South Commission) is that if African countries want to develop in freedom, they must first put their own people, their own money and their own resources to maximum use. Another problem is that when our countries talk of external cooperation partnerships, they only think of the North. They never consider the possibility of South–South cooperation, say between southern Africa and Latin America.

Cassam: In 1995, four years after the above interview, Nyerere and the highly respected Tanzanian permanent representative to the United Nations in Geneva, Amir Jamal, successfully negotiated with the Swiss authorities the establishment of the South Centre in that city. The main goal of this unique intergovernmental institution was to promote solidarity and cooperation among all the countries of the South and to strengthen their collective presence in the economic and commercial arenas of the UN. As the South Centre's first executive director, Mwalimu chose India's Manmohan Singh, now prime minister of his country.

If the never-ending, never-completed Doha Development Round concocted by the World Trade Organisation, also based in Geneva, has achieved anything, it is surely the opportunity to teach the South some very important lessons about the North–South gap or abyss. Since the Doha exercise began in 2001, the emergent, the developing and the very poor members of the South have seen at first-hand – and under laboratory conditions – the importance of the expert advice and analysis available at their own centre in order to face the Northern bulldozers disguised as 'trade talks and development rounds'.

As I write, the leading countries of the South – China, India, Brazil, South Africa and Venezuela – have at last got their act together to put into place some of the concrete forms of South–South cooperation that Nyerere talked of years ago.

Yes, now we see the birth of a new god, one called capitalism, which supposedly has all the answers … At present we are living a moment of deception. But the conditions being created on the ground by this euphoria over capitalism gives me reason to believe that, in about ten years or so, the ideal of socialism will return – and more forcefully than before.

Cassam: It is difficult, this side of the worst crisis since 1929 – or this side of the banking binge, to be more precise – to recall the gross, self-congratulatory triumphalism that gripped the minds of so many citizens and leaders when the Soviet Union collapsed and the Berlin Wall was brought down in 1989. Some very bizarre exaggerations were invented to promote the theory that three saints, Reagan, Thatcher and Milton Friedman, held up the capitalist sky over all our heads, for which we should be eternally grateful. And in any case, there was no alternative...

Two years later, in 1991, Nyerere tells the Madrid journalist not to get carried away and even more, not to believe that the purpose is a society based on General Motors. He then goes on to point out that unregulated bouts of over-indulgence will inevitably lead to severe hangovers in about ten years, and then what some call a mistake, that is, the ideal of a just society, socialism, will be back. And perhaps he is right.

I belong to a dying breed, one that resists reneging on its own ideals.

Cassam: This is pure Mwalimu, laughing quietly at himself, using self-deprecating but gentle irony to drive home a very unpopular point in 1991: history never ends, it only repeats itself. He is saying it is better to stand firm by your beliefs, if you have beliefs, not to follow the herd and not to deny reality – and all of this has nothing to do with ideology.

Reflecting with Nyerere on people-centred leadership

Marjorie Mbilinyi

'Who are we? Who am I?'

When talking about leadership, we need to ask three questions: leadership of what? Of whom? And for what? We are situated within a particular context, one which will be understood differently depending in part on our own positions within society.

How do we position ourselves in this moment of history, when Africa is undergoing another 'scramble for Africa', heightened by the global fiscal and economic crisis of 2008–09 and when eastern and western powers are competing between and among themselves for natural resources and military and political hegemony? With unheard of violence perpetrated against women and children, there is no neutrality here, no middle ground.

Leadership ethics are relevant not only to formal 'big P' politics – as found in central and local government and in political parties – but also to the way leaders conduct themselves within civil society organisations, including activist groups and the media, as well as within the commercial and corporate sector.

My chapter is informed by Nyerere's thoughts on colonialism and post-colonialism. It is also highly informed by my participation in women's struggles for equality, justice and social transformation in Tanzania and Africa, beginning in 1967, and our efforts to build a transformative feminist movement (Kitunga and Mbilinyi 2006; Kitunga 2007a and 2007b; Mbilinyi 2007). I remain a youth of the 1960s and a 'child of Nyerere'. As a teenager, I was already active in the civil rights movement in the USA, and in 1967, at 23 years old, I became a wife, a citizen of Tanzania, bore my first daughter, was active in the struggle for 'socialism and self-reliance' and challenged patriarchy at home and at work.

In those days we were highly critical of Nyerere's contradictions and government actions, but I continue to recognise and appreciate Mwalimu's steadfast love for the people of Tanzania and Africa, his commitment to equity, justice and freedom, his enduring learning attitude and openness to new ideas and his political savvy. Mwalimu is sorely missed at this crisis moment in African and human history. We look for similar inspirational leadership in today's youth, who will carry on the struggle for an equitable, just and transformed world.

This chapter is thus written with certain assumptions in mind that ought to be set forth from the start. First, I believe that the major issue today is neither corruption nor competent governance – these phenomena require explanation. The major issue remains that of exploitative and oppressive structures and relations of production and reproduction, which are over-determined by the further strengthening of imperialist relations. These imperialist relations underlie such problems as debt, unequal terms of trade, foreign exchange strangulation, and the growing power of multinational corporations within Tanzania's economy, and that of Africa as a whole. Imperialist relations interact with capitalist, patriarchal, racist, traditionalist and fundamentalist structures, systems and relations – they cannot, nor should they be, separated from each other.

Corruption and the lack of patriotic leadership has increased during the last 20 some years, but not in a vacuum. An enabling environment was created for corruption, individualism and compradorial tendencies by neoliberal ideology and macroeconomic reforms which successfully took a dominant position in Tanzania – and much of the rest of Africa – in the mid-1980s. I propose therefore that the major challenge we face is the abolition of unjust, exploitative and oppressive structures and systems, and the creation and maintenance of structures and systems within the economy and polity characterised by equality and justice at all levels, beginning in the home and family and extending to the regional and global levels.

To cite Mwalimu Nyerere in his 1986 speech to the Nigerian Institute of International Affairs:

Yet policy mistakes by our young governments, or the existence of shameful corruption in many countries, is not sufficient
explanation for Africa's current economic condition. Although
all African governments differ in ideology, policy, and structure
... all countries have suffered a similar kind of economic regres-
sion and now face similar problems.

I believe that the basic explanation for Africa's present economic condition lies in the fact that no African country has yet
managed to shake off the neo-colonial hold of industrialized
nations over our economies... Africa therefore continues to
have an unequal dependency relationship with the developed
nations – mostly former colonial powers.

(Nyerere 1986, pp. 8-9)

In the same speech, Mwalimu reminds us of the historical context
leading up to the present situation, which was defined by the
struggles of African peoples against colonialism and racism (and,
I would add, against sexism):

Our people's demand for independence, however, derived its
major strength from their demand for human dignity and freedom. They wanted to govern themselves, in their own interests.
And while they were demanding improvements in their conditions of life and in the provision of social services, they also
wanted freedom and peace in their villages and towns and in
their own lives.

(Nyerere 1986, pp. 5-6)

Mwalimu then goes on: '... on balance, it cannot be said that
we have fulfilled our people's hopes for democracy and Human
Rights' (Nyerere 1986, p. 6). That, I believe, ought to be the main
focus of our deliberations today, whereby democracy is understood broadly to refer to participatory development and participatory democracy in which all women and men participate equally in making key decisions on resource allocations, at all levels.
In other words, they all lead – and they benefit equally – where
there is no systematic discrimination against one or another social
group on any grounds whatsoever, thus realising the people's
demand for human dignity and freedom.

While referring to individual demands for freedom and dignity, Mwalimu also emphasised the collective nature of these
demands, and argued that the African people can only realise real

democracy and freedom by uniting together so as to fight against 'neocolonialism' – i.e., imperialism – and struggling instead for equitable, just development and economic liberation.

In the next section of this chapter, I will explore what leadership ethics means, highlighting the central question of positionality. Context issues are further examined in the third section from the point of view of the most oppressed and exploited group in Tanzanian society. The final section seeks to answer the question: How do we shape a people-centred leadership which is accountable first to the people – meaning women, men and children – and not capitalist investors and 'donors' nor local money merchants who pay for political parties and their elections?

What do leadership ethics mean?

From a transformative feminist point of view, leadership ethics centres around the question of positionality and identity, as well as the question of transparency and accountability (Kitunga and Mbilinyi 2006). What is the position of the leader, in terms of gender, class, rural–urban location, ethnicity and race, and nation and region in the present context summarised above? With whom does the leader (or the collective leadership) identify? We refer here to positionality and identity in practice, not in rhetoric. The measure of a leader's positionality and identity will be that leader's actions, behaviour and thoughts in both private and public life. Government leaders in turn will be judged not by their policy statements but by their actual implementation of policies, and resource allocations which reach the end user; for example, the nurse and the patient or the teacher and the student.

Who is the leader accountable to? Again, accountability is measured by actions, not by mere rhetoric. How does the leader respond to the conflicting demands of different social categories in our society in the context of the dominant relations of power and ownership of wealth? In whose interests does this leader serve, the big corporate investors and the global, multilateral and bilateral agencies which support them or the exploited and oppressed majority? Does the leader support conservative forces which seek to maintain the status quo with respect to gender, class, race and national relations, or revolutionary forces which seek to promote participatory democracy and development through the emancipation of all oppressed and exploited groups? Again, the question needs asking not only of government and political leaders, but also the leaders of a media house, an activist organisation, a student movement, a commercial enterprise and the leaders of a nuclear and extended family or clan.

Another dimension of leadership ethics is the level of courage and commitment of a given leader. Is the leader prepared to stand up and voice their position on a given issue, regardless of the consequences, even when it means taking a minority position and challenging the might of the power structure within a given party, the government, a civil society organisation or even a commercial company? Is the leader prepared to defend the interests of the dominated, oppressed and exploited majority vis-à-vis an increasingly voracious, wealthy and powerful minority at the local, national, regional and global levels? Will the leader speak truth to power, without fear? And are we prepared to support them?

In the views of many Tanzanians today, elected leaders – including most members of parliament (MPs) and district councillors – are a bunch of sheep, afraid to speak out on injustice and inequalities, afraid to stand out alone and separate from the pack. Most elected leaders have no intention of serving the interests of the exploited majority. They bought their positions with their own big money or provided by their commercial benefactors, and have taken political power so as to enrich themselves, the very opposite of what Mwalimu's philosophy called for, and exactly what he warned the people against.

Where do people-centred leaders come from – the kind of committed leaders that Mwalimu spoke about – who are wholly and completely dedicated to serving the majority of the people? I will argue here that they are not born as people-centred leaders, but rather that they are constructed in part by their birth and upbringing and by the social forces which define their circumstances. They are constructed by the structures and systems of organising and leadership which are created and sustained within our respective families, communities, civil society organisations (including religious institutions, advocacy NGOs and grassroots movements), political parties and the government itself. Top-down dictatorial

81

leaders on the other hand are constructed by bureaucratic, hierarchical structures and systems of organising and leadership.

Here I would like to distinguish between leader-centred groups and group-centred leaders, drawing on the inspiration of Ella Baker, a leader of the civil rights movement against racism and classism in the United States in the 1940s through to the 1970s (Grant 1998) and the experiences of collective, participatory decision-making in some feminist and women's organisations, including that of the Tanzania Gender Networking Programme (TGNP).

Leader-centred groups – the vast majority in modern capitalist society – are characterised by the leadership of charismatic individuals with whom the organisation or movement or party is identified. In a literal sense, these groups will be known as so-and-so's organisation, completely identified with a person, and not the collectivity contained within. A hierarchy of power is created based on top-down decision-making, such that the majority of staff and members are excluded from participation in significant decisions about policy and resource allocations. Should that leader be removed, silenced or have left of their own accord, such organisations often fall apart. Most government structures in Africa are also organised in this way, where ideology, force and repression are relied upon to maintain the leader and party in power, as well as the granting of patronage and favours so as to maintain the support of specific power and pressure groups.

Group-centred leaders, in contrast, are grounded within their organisations, institutions or movements. The groups, organisations and movements they lead are identified not by a particular individual, but rather by the collectivity and its vision and mission. Decisions are made in a collective and participatory way through animation (participatory dialogue and debate), which though time-consuming ensures that everyone concerned understands what the decision is about and what the implications are, and will be prepared later to abide by the decision of the majority, if not the consensus of all.

Group-centred leadership also connotes a learning organisation or institution which continually strengthens and enriches its understanding of the current reality of struggle and development because its dynamics allow for continual reflection, criticism, self-criticism and counter-criticism. People-centred leaders are nourished within group-centred leadership structures, and are mentored, supported and corrected when they begin to lose their way – be it in terms of positionality, identity, transparency or accountability. Corrective mechanisms are in place to immediately censure inappropriate behaviour and actions. Everyone has an interest in ensuring that openness, transparency and accountability prevail because the organisation or movement is 'owned' by its members or collectivity. They identify with the organisation and the organisation identifies with them, and not with one individual.

Of course, this is an ideal, one which group-centred leadership organisations strive to achieve, but it does make a difference.

Having explored the meaning of leadership ethics in this section, I would like to analyse the contextual issues and circumstances in which we are carrying out this public dialogue today, the context behind which also partly determines what kind of leaders we get, what kind of organisations and government (centrally, locally and globally) and what kind of families. These issues also shape the forms of resistance and struggle which are emerging in Tanzania, and the growing power of the contentious organisation and discourse among the exploited and oppressed women and men in the rural areas and in towns.

Contextual issues in neoliberal globalisation

At the broad level, today as we discuss leadership ethics we are located within a particularly ugly moment of 'his'story, one very definitely a 'his'story dominated by imperial, capitalist, patriarchal, white supremacist and traditionalist structures of power and wealth. Global politics is heavily determined by the decisions and actions of a few powerful, largely white, men situated in advanced capitalist countries and their collaborators and compradors in the increasingly subjugated and underdeveloped world, none more marginalised and subjugated than Africa. The imperial capitalist forces are frantic in their efforts to survive what is in reality a moment of crisis in capitalism. Instruments of force and repression are relied upon, including outright warfare and military domination. Moreover, the military industrial complex has become one of the most powerful, if not the most powerful, sector of modern capitalist society. The capitalist economy

83

depends on the military industrial complex, with myriad consequences in terms of research, ideology and discourse, including the discursive construction of particular forms of masculinity and femininity in a militarised society and world.

Imperial capitalism also relies on ideological instruments to rule and dominate, including patriarchal values and beliefs, and here the battle for the minds, aspirations, emotions and dreams of women, men and especially youth and children looms large. The convergence between far-right politics, undemocratic governance, religious fundamentalism and market fundamentalism has increased throughout the world. It informs dominant discourse in the media and popular culture (including the mindless popular corporate culture of cinema and song). The politics of HIV/AIDS (condoms or abstinence) are one expression of this ideological struggle. Another is the transformation of African universities from radical centres of excellence characterised by debate and innovative research in the 1960s, 1970s and 1980s to today's market-mainstreamed centres of mediocrity dependent on foreign donations of money and ideas.

In the 1960s and 1970s, African governments – and none more so than Tanzania under Mwalimu Nyerere – sought to challenge western imperial hegemony and to support popular movements for decolonisation, for social equality and for justice for all. Whatever their personal inclinations, Tanzanian leaders of government and political parties were shaped by strong ideological forces and institutional mechanisms so as to abide by a certain level of respect for the 'common people'. Wealth where it existed was not flaunted and in real terms the gap between the powerful and wealthy and the poor in Tanzania was among the lowest in Africa. Many leaders actively sought to serve their nation and the African continent, and they and the Tanzanian people had pride in who they were – Africans and Tanzanians. Regardless of differences in gender, class, race, ethnicity, religion and rural–urban location, there was a real sense of Tanzanian pride.

What is not understood is the degree to which this nationalist identity was constructed through the actions and thoughts of grassroots women politicians and activists, women who merged their struggles for individual dignity with that of a collective struggle for national autonomy and dignity as an African people.

It was 'TANU women' (Tanganyika African National Union) who forged alliances across ethnic and religious boundaries, who promoted Kiswahili as the medium of political discourse, who used local African cultural forms such as women's songs and dance groups to energise the nationalist struggle and make it their own (Geiger 1997). Women anti-colonial agitators exemplified courage in the face of tremendous odds. They defied the power of the colonial state and the power of African patriarchy. They successfully fashioned non-violent methods with which to face colonial police forces and were able to organise huge demonstrations with 40,000 people or more.

Door-to-door campaigns to raise funds and increase party membership were led and composed by women members, and this provided the foundation for a national liberation movement not defined by political party politics. Its horizons were far broader, the very construction of a free and independent nation.

As argued by Susan Geiger in her life histories of TANU women activists (1997 and 2005), this nationalist identity was strong enough to survive not only the first 20 years of independence, with the many achievements in real economic growth and a better quality of life for all in the late 1960s and 1970s, but also the hard times of the 1980s. However, we must ask today, how much is left of that sense of pride in being Tanzanian and in being an African people?

What do we have today? Horrendous gaps between the rich and the poor, the powerful and the powerless, with wealth and power being openly flaunted in the faces of the excluded majority. In less than 10 years Tanzania has witnessed the 'mallisation' of its society and economy. Shopping centres spring up with fences, gates and guards to lock out the poor majority, and an increasing number of the wealthy and the powerful now live in gated communities – also protected by fences, guards and dogs – and thus Tanzanian society begins to resemble that of apartheid South Africa, a system which its leaders once sought to demolish. Rich children attend elite private schools, while the poor majority attend low-quality government and community schools that resemble, superficially, the old 'native' schools for Africans of the colonial period. I say superficially because those colonial native schools did at least teach their students how to read and write, whereas today how many primary school leavers remain functionally illiterate?

Now I want to dig down deeper to explore the view from below of the context in which a growing number of Tanzanians live and struggle. Imagine you are a 12-year-old girl who has been sexually abused by your uncle, father, teacher or priest; a 16-year-old pregnant girl, pulled out of school and married off by her father to an old man without a choice; or an 11-year-old girl whose auntie brings her to town, promising her an education, and instead she winds up a domestic servant in a stranger's house, raped by the 'father' and the 'sons', thrown out of the house when she gets pregnant by the mistress of the house, and left to her own devices only to become a commercial sex worker.

Or, imagine you are a female casual labourer on a tea plantation who makes barely Tsh 2,000 (Tanzanian shillings) (equivalent to about US$1.50) a day plucking tea with a baby on her back, from sun up to sun down. After five years' work she asks about regular employment and is fired. Or imagine a 32-year-old woman in her sixth delivery who dies because she didn't have the money to pay for transport to the district hospital, the only place where emergency delivery care would be found. What is the view of the collectivity of Tanzanian mothers, the vast majority of whom have experienced the death of at least one child because of malnutrition, the lack of safe, clean water, the lack of quality healthcare, the lack of food security and the lack of a sustainable livelihood?

And, I ask you, what kind of leaders do we have in this nation who are so oblivious of the fact that systematically, every hour of every day, at least one woman dies because of complications in pregnancy and childbirth? What kind of leaders do we have in a nation where more than 40 per cent of young girls' first experience of sex is violent – involving incest or rape in the majority of cases by someone close to them – or where, more than 47 years after independence, the economy still depends on the head-loads of women to provide fuel, water and foodstuffs for their families and communities? And what of the hand hoe to feed this nation, a nation where the national economy continues to exploit systematically the unpaid labour of women and children to provide basic sustenance and the reproduction of their families and communities, and by extension, the labour force of the economy? Added to this, we actually have an official government policy called 'Home Based Care' which exploits this same unpaid labour to provide care and treatment for people living with HIV (PLHIVs), with little or no resource allocations to support them.

What kind of leadership in government – but also in development and economic studies – do we have which contemplates without shame the fact that the most common form of employment right now for young women is commercial sex, along with domestic work and bar work? This is a government which talks about providing jobs and economic empowerment, but in practice demolishes the stalls and by extension the means of the livelihoods of *mama ntilies* (women foodstuff sellers) and their brother *wamachingas* (street hawkers) in the *bomoa bomoa* campaign. What kind of leadership ethics do we have from the point of view of the *mama nitilies*, the raped girl child, or the girl student who is systematically discriminated against in school, home and the community, not only on the basis of her sex, but also her class and her rural or poor urban location?

Although these are individual stories, they reflect systematic discrimination, systematic male violence against women and girls and systematic strategies to keep women in their place as the most exploited and oppressed group in our society. Underlying these stories is the state's perpetuation of customary laws, for example, which rob women of their rights to property and the fruits of their labour; the state's absolute failure to develop a coherent employment strategy for all so as to ensure that every woman – and man – has access to a sustainable livelihood with dignity and a liveable income; and the state policy of privatisation and cost-sharing in social services, which denies citizens their rights to primary healthcare, safe, clean water, and basic education.

Where does people-centred leadership come from?

At the beginning of this chapter, I argued that people-centred leadership is constructed and leaders of this nature are not born that way. Alternative organising and leadership styles which foster and reward women and men leaders who are patriotic, committed, dedicated, democratic and participatory in action are essential. They are desperately needed to lead social movements for change, as well as to lead other institutions and organisations in civil society and within political parties and government. On the other hand, strong and powerful social movements are needed to successfully demand the people-centred leadership of elected officials and a free and independent media.

Transformative pedagogy is also a way to promote people-centred leadership, whereby each student feels compelled to do their best for the common good as well as for their own individual achievement. Participatory methods and a philosophy of learning, organising and action research have been developed within the animation conceptual framework, which is also referred to by some as 'participatory action research' or Paulo Freire's 'pedagogy of the oppressed'. Several activist organisations in Tanzania, for example, have adopted animation as the way they organise themselves, and also how they facilitate dialogue and debate among the communities in which they work (see Mbilinyi in Mbilinyi et al 2003). A basic assumption of animation is that the role of a facilitator is to creatively listen and to learn from the oppressed, exploited groups with whom they work and to create an interactive process of experiential learning whereby people assess their situation, analyse the basic causes and act to change their circumstances on their own behalf. In this case the educator does not teach but rather facilitates a mutual learning process. When applied to the context of a political party or a movement, the political leaders do not preach and they do not command compliance; instead, they first go to live and learn from the people and later articulate the popular demands of the people, namely the oppressed and exploited women, men and children.

Mwalimu's thoughts on liberating education were inseparably linked with his conception of a more participatory political and development process. For example, in his 'Education for self reliance' (1968) he stated:

> It would thus be a gross misinterpretation of our needs to suggest that the educational system should be designed to produce robots, which work hard but never question what the leaders in Government or TANU are doing and saying... Our Government and our Party must always be responsible to the

people, and must always consist of representatives – spokes-men and servants of the people.

(Lema et al 2004)

In 'Adult education and development' (Nyerere 1978), Mwalimu placed the liberation of human beings as the centre and ration-ale for development, and not the production of goods. Warning against paternalistic attitudes and top-down structures of leader-ship, he also argued that:

Man [note the use of the term 'man'] can only liberate himself or develop himself. He cannot be liberated or developed by another. For Man makes himself... The expansion of his own consciousness, and therefore of his power over himself, his environment, and his society, must therefore ultimately be what we mean by development.

(Nyerere 1978, p. 135)

This calls for a transformative pedagogy, in Mwalimu's words, 'the first function of adult education is to inspire both a desire for change, and an understanding that change is possible' (Nyerere 1978, p. 137). What is included?:

It includes training, but is much more than training. It includes what is generally called 'agitation' but it is much more than that. It includes organization and mobilization, but it goes beyond them to make them purposeful.

(Nyerere 1978, p. 138)

According to Mwalimu, political activists and educators 'are not politically neutral; by the nature of what they are doing they can-not be. For what they are doing will affect how men look at the society in which they live, and how they seek to use it or change it... Adult education is thus a highly political activity. Politicians ... therefore ... do not always welcome real adult education' (Nyerere 1978, p. 138).

Mwalimu's concept was of a contentious education process which promoted revolutionary struggle, while at the same time fostering high standards of excellence in scholarship (Lema et al 2006):

Education ought to enable whoever acquires it to fight against oppression.

... we have not succeeded in liberating ourselves mentally, nor in having self-confidence, nor in selecting that which is most suitable to our objective conditions instead of continuing to ape the systems of other people whose economy and mode of life is totally different from ours.

Source: Musoma resolution directive on the implementation of 'Education for self reliance' (1974)

... a University can only fulfill its functions if it is the hub of, and a stimulus for, the kind of scientific thinking which is a necessary preliminary to constructive action ... a University – which in this context means its staff and students – must have untrammeled freedom to think, and to exchange thoughts, even if the thinking leads some of its members to become unorthodox in their conclusions...

In addition to the University's duties to the society, there is a particular obligation on University students as a result of their having what are in developing countries exceptional educational opportunities... In 1970, and in the context of a country committed to building socialism, I described this obligation as being a willingness to give service to the community 'without demanding further privileges from the community.' Whether Tanzania is still an aspiring socialist country or not, I stand by that statement.

... no government is completely free in its choices ... [it cannot] decide to privatise Universities (that is, to leave the provision of tertiary education to 'the market') without abandoning even the shadow of a commitment both to equal opportunity for all its citizens, and even to genuine university education ... I fail to see how the prime purpose of making a profit is consistent with the academic freedom and excellence which is an intrinsic part of being a University.

Source: Address at the 25th anniversary of the University of Dar es Salaam (1 July 1995)

I wish to close with a passionate speech which Mwalimu made to teachers in Dar es Salaam in 1969, 'The job of teachers is revolution', which is befitting for this commemoration of his life (Lema et al 2006):

When we talk of change or revolution in education, teachers begin arguing: 'Oh! You will lower standards!' But whose standards? They are colonial standards – and of how much use have they been to us? If these standards were good and relevant to our situation, we would not be talking of weakness and poverty today. We must be able to see what is good for ourselves and only in this way can we change. You teachers therefore must accept to be revolutionary teachers, not teachers to make people go to sleep.

Even if you are working in the village your job is to bring about African Revolution. You are carrying out your duty for the whole of Africa. Because history has given us Tanzania, we have to eradicate weakness and poverty in Tanzania. But we are not working for Tanzania alone. We are also working for Africa because of the suffering we have experienced as Africans.

You are working for Africa and secondly you are playing your part in a world-wide revolution. A situation where the rich exploit the poor will go. All exploiters will be dealt with in the world.

If you as teachers do not lead the poor African, when that day comes when there will be one to lead them out of poverty and misery you should agree to step down and accept to be led by an army of poor Africans. And I will be happy to see you trodden upon because you were useless as leaders. You must lead the poor...

References

Geiger, S. (1997) *TANU Women: Gender and Culture in the Making of Tanganyikan Nationalism*, 1955–1965, Oxford, James Currey

Geiger, S. (2005) *Wanawake wa TANU: Jinsia na Utamaduni katika Kujenga Uzalendo Tanganyika: 1955–1965*, Tanzania Gender Networking Programme (TGNP)

Grant, J. (1998) *Ella Baker: Freedom Bound*, New York, John Wiley & Sons

Kitunga, D. (2007a) 'Challenges of feminist organising and movement building', *Ulingo wa Jinsia*, July–September, Tanzania Gender Networking Programme (TGNP)

Kitunga, D. (2007b) 'Vuguvugu la Ukombozi wa Wanawake Kimapinduzi na Changamoto Zake', *Ulingo wa Jinsia*, special issue

Kitunga, D. and Mbilinyi, M. (2006) 'Notes on transformative feminism', *Ulingo wa Jinsia*, July–September, Tanzania Gender Networking Programme (TGNP)

Lema, E., Mbilinyi, M. and Rajani, R. (eds) (2004) *Nyerere on Education*, Dar es Salaam, HaKiElimu and E & D Limited

Lema, E., Omari, I. and Rajani, R. (eds) (2006) *Nyerere on Education II*, Dar es Salaam, HaKiElimu and E & D Limited

Mbilinyi, M. (2007) 'Achievements and challenges in feminist participatory organising and movement building', *Ulingo wa Jinsia*, July–September, Tanzania Gender Networking Programme (TGNP)

Mbilinyi, M., Rusimbi, M., Chachage, C.S.L., and Kitunga, D. (eds) (2003) *Activist Voices: Feminist Struggles for an Alternative World*, Dar es Salaam, Tanzania Gender Networking Programme (TGNP) and E & D Limited

Nyerere, J.K. (1968) 'Education for self reliance', in Lema et al 2004

Nyerere, J.K. (1969) 'The job of teachers is revolution', in Lema et al 2006

Nyerere, J.K. (1974) Musoma resolution directive on the implementation of 'Education for self reliance', in Lema et al 2006

Nyerere, J.K. (1978) 'Adult education and development', in Hall, B. and Kidd J.R. (eds) *Adult Learning: A Design for Action*, London, Pergamon Press

Nyerere, J.K. (1986) 'Reflections on Africa and its future', address at the Nigerian Institution of International Affairs, 8 December, mimeo

Nyerere, J.K. (1995) 'Address at the 25th anniversary of the University of Dar es Salaam' (1 July), in Lema et al 2006

Nyerere's vision of economic development

Faustin Kamuzora

Introduction

After gaining independence in the early 1960s, many African countries tried a variety of economic policies to bring economic development to their citizenry. Under the leadership of Mwalimu Nyerere, the government of Tanzania, initially on the mainland but later for the entire republic, invoked economic policies which aimed to raise the living standard of all Tanzanians.

The main objective of this chapter is to demonstrate that the first phase government under Mwalimu had an impeccable desire and commitment to reducing the level of poverty. It provides an historical account of economic policies that were employed in the struggle to bring economic development to Tanzanians. Since the majority of the citizenry lived in rural areas, economic policies accorded rural development high priority. The policies had mixed success but their underlying philosophy of building an egalitarian society cannot be challenged.

Development efforts after independence

Immediately after independence the Tanganyikan government under Mwalimu Nyerere declared three development problems, namely, poverty, disease and ignorance. Using Tanganyikan and donor resources, the Development Plan for Tanganyika 1961/62–63/64 aimed at creating an enabling environment for rural development that would fight these problems. Accordingly, the first development budget under this plan allocated funding to the major sectors as follows: agriculture (24 per cent), communication, power and works (28.8 per cent), and education (13.7 per cent).

This budgetary allocation clearly depicts the commitment of the government of the day to spearheading rural development. The agricultural sector that supported the livelihood of the majority of people of Tanganyika was allocated nearly a quarter of the development budget. In the same vein, communication, power and works – infrastructural sectors that support rural development – were also allocated a lion's share of the budget. The education sector – important for fighting ignorance – received the next biggest allocation.

Similarly, the first Five-Year Plan (1964 to 1969) aimed at reducing poverty through an improvement approach in developing the agricultural sector, but in the long run it employed a transformation approach. The latter approach would involve settlement schemes where modern machinery would be provided and, if possible, irrigation facilities. Also, the plan encouraged private enterprise for economic development but cautioned that it would contradict government intention to expand cooperatives and government activities in commerce and industry, as well as in agriculture (Government of Tanganyika 1964).

The growth of the economy was too low to achieve the targeted objectives of poverty reduction. Between 1960/61 and 1967 the economic growth rate was 4.3–5 per cent per annum. With an increase in the population growth rate of 2.7 per cent, the real economic growth of 2.3 per cent per annum was not sufficient to bring about tangible economic development. A drop in the price of sisal, a lack of experts, poor implementation of the first development plan, and a lot of resources being expended on settlement schemes were the other factors that lay behind the country's failure to meet its rural development goals.

The Arusha Declaration and rural development

These factors prompted the government to change its approach to rural development by announcing the Arusha Declaration in 1967; it resulted in the nationalisation of many pillars of the economy. Its original objective of state ownership of the major means of the economy was to ensure that the corporate sector of the economy was in national hands. Before nationalisation control of the pillars of the economy was either in the hands of foreign investors or the minorities that enjoyed business dominance at independence. At that time the economic policy assumed that public enterprises would perform in an environment of market accountability, management autonomy and incentives for efficiency.

The focus, given the nature of Tanzanian society, was still on rural development. People were encouraged to live and work on a cooperative basis in organised villages. The idea was to extend traditional values and the responsibilities around kinship to Tanzania as a whole. A policy booklet on *Socialism and Rural Development* was released in 1968. It clarified the way the Arusha Declaration was to implement a rural development strategy in order to fight poverty. The following excerpts from Nyerere's *Ujamaa: Essays on Socialism* (1968) summarise the gist of the Arusha Declaration on rural development:

It is particularly important that we should now understand the connection between freedom, development, and discipline, because our national policy of creating socialist villages throughout the rural areas depends upon it. For we have known for a very long time that development had to go on in the rural areas, and that this required cooperative activities by the people...

When we tried to promote rural development in the past, we sometimes spent huge sums of money on establishing a Settlement, and supplying it with modern equipment, and social services, as well as often providing it with a management hierarchy ... All too often, we persuaded people to go into new settlements by promising them that they could quickly grow rich there, or that Government would give them services and equipment which they could not hope to receive either in the towns or in their traditional farming places. In very few cases was any ideology involved; we thought and talked in terms of greatly increased output, and of things being provided for the settlers.

What we were doing, in fact, was thinking of development in terms of things, and not of people ... As a result, there have been very many cases where heavy capital investment has resulted in no increase in output where the investment has been wasted. And in most of the officially sponsored or supported schemes, the majority of people who went to settle lost their enthusiasm, and either left the scheme altogether, or failed to carry out the orders of the outsiders who were put in charge – and who were not themselves involved in the success or failure of the project.

It is important, therefore, to realise that the policy of Ujamaa Vijijini is not intended to be merely a revival of the old settlement schemes under another name. The Ujamaa village is a new conception, based on the post Arusha Declaration understanding that what we need to develop is people, not things, and that people can only develop themselves...

Ujamaa villages are intended to be socialist organisations created by the people, and governed by those who live and work in them. They cannot be created from outside, nor governed from outside. No one can be forced into an Ujamaa village, and no official – at any level – can go and tell the members of an Ujamaa village what they should do together, and what they should continue to do as individual farmers.

It is important that these things should be thoroughly understood. It is also important that the people should not be persuaded to start an Ujamaa village by promises of the things which will be given to them if they do so. A group of people must decide to start an Ujamaa village because they have understood that only through this method can they live and develop in dignity and freedom, receiving the full benefits of their cooperative endeavour...

Unless the purpose and socialist ideology of an Ujamaa village is understood by the members from the beginning – at least to some extent it will not survive the early difficulties. For no one can guarantee that there will not be a crop failure in the first or second year – there might be a drought or floods. And the greater self-discipline which is necessary when working in a community will only be forthcoming if the people understand what they are doing and why.

As we can see from the above excerpt, there was a commitment to raising basic living standards (and an opposition to conspicuous consumption and large private wealth). The socialism Mwalimu Nyerere believed in was 'people-centred'. To him, humanness in its fullest sense rather than wealth creation must come first. Societies become better places through the development of people rather than just the gearing up of production for the sake of production. In addition, the aspiration was to attain a self-reliant, egalitarian and human-centred society where all members have equal rights and equal opportunities; in which all can live in peace with their neighbours without suffering or imposing injustice, being exploited or exploiting; and in which all have a gradually increasing basic level of material welfare before any individual lives in luxury (Nyerere 1968, p. 340).

One has to acknowledge that these moral standards cannot be challenged even in today's world where an unregulated open market philosophy and a number of post-modernist tendencies are not empowering poor people to improve their socio-economic wellbeing. As seen from the policy on socialism and rural development, 'The development of a country is brought about by people, not by money. Money, and the wealth it represents, is the result and not the basis of development' (Nyerere 1968, p. 243). Similarly, it emphatically delineated what are the prerequisites of development. These were identified as people, land, good policies and good leadership.

Thus, with the advantage of evidence from a number of Asian latecomers in the development arena, I believe that of the four prerequisites, people and good leadership are the most critical missing parts of the development jigsaw. This is because there are a number of countries and societies in today's world which have managed to attain very high socio-economic development without large land masses. Similarly, good leadership will definitely promote good policies and in normal thinking, leaders are usually a reflection of the society they are coming from. As Nyerere's analogy attests, if you fetch a bowl of water from a dirty well, the water in the bowl will also be dirty.

Improvement of the Human Development Index

Despite the fact that some of the economic policies under Nyerere resulted in a reduction in productivity in some sectors, his focus on human development and self-reliance did bring some success in other areas of socio-economic indicators as shown by the Human Development Index (HDI). The HDIs have been calculated annually by UNDP since 1960. Various authorities such as UNDP and the World Bank have indicated that the ranking of

Tanzania for some socio-economic development indicators has declined in recent years.

The contrary was true under Mwalimu Nyerere's government when the HDI indices were improving. One good example is the illiteracy rate, which was 90 per cent in 1960. At its lowest levels in the mid-1980s it declined to 10 per cent but figures for 2000–07 indicate that it had risen to around 28 per cent. In the so-called knowledge-based economy of today's world, illiteracy is one of the severest constraints on socio-economic development because illiteracy reduces the chances of an individual exploring their potential.

Rural development strategies: 1970s and early 1980s

As seen above, efforts to curb poverty in Tanzania started right after independence in 1961. Several strategies were employed to bring about rural development. These included the establishment of settlement schemes. In the mid-1970s, the villagisation programme was also a means that the government thought could bring about rapid rural development after the slow pace of forming Ujamaa villages (Woods 1975 and Ellman 1975). In addition, in the1970s, government functions were decentralised.

Decentralisation in the 1970s

Three major problems emerged during the period 1961–71 due to the organisational structure that Tanzania had inherited at independence. The first problem was the lack of coordination between the four organisational systems, namely, the ministries, local government, the then single political party, TANU, and the planning structure. Because of the overriding role that TANU, in particular, and the planning system played in the development process of Tanzania, the ministries and local government were frequently confronted with policies and plans that could not be realistically implemented for lack of manpower, funds, equipment, organisation and decision-making powers.

The second problem was the lack of coordination within individual systems, especially those responsible for government administration and planning. Because of the more or less autonomous behaviour of ministries responsible for the various economic and social sectors, three minor problems were created. First, it was difficult to plan and implement projects which involved more than one ministry and so one found agricultural projects without transport or marketing facilities, settlement schemes without extension staff or social services, etc. Second, there was very little coordination between different projects in the same area, that is to say there was no regional integrated development planning. And third, because of the tendency to consider development in sectoral rather than in spatial terms, relatively little attention was given to regional differences in resource endowments and needs, resulting in imbalanced regional development and the accentuation of regional inequalities.

The third major problem was that powers of decision-making were over-centralised within political, planning and ministerial organisations. When the desire for national control and planning became dominant, especially after independence, the effects of over-centralisation of power in ministerial headquarters in Dar es Salaam were to handicap the planning and implementation of projects on the spot, and to alienate the general public from the development process (Kamuzora 2002).

Government reorganisation was in response to these problems and was aimed at the decentralisation of a large part of the responsibility for planning and implementing development programmes and at the dissolution of the traditional ministerial structure.

Regional integrated development programmes

The trend towards decentralisation resulted in the formulation of various regional integrated development programmes (RIDEPs). When the call for assistance for RIDEPs was made in 1972, the administrative level responsible for people's development was the region. The regions therefore became natural focuses both in the planning and the implementation of development interventions.

This wave of integrated rural development became the new fashion for both multilateral and bilateral development assistance agencies. By the financial year 1974/75 all the then 20 regions in the country had received assured pledges of donor support from foreign donors except for the Rukwa region. However, by the late 1970s, the government in collaboration with various donors was implementing only 10 RIDEPS in the country. Those located in Kigoma, Mwanza, Shinyanga and Tabora were under the funding and management of the World Bank; others included Tanga (the Federal Republic of Germany), Kilimanjaro (Japan), Iringa (EEC), Arusha (USAID) (Ngasongwa 1988). Kigoma's RIDEP was later abandoned by the World Bank and subsequently 'inherited' by NORAD. Rukwa's RIDEP was also funded by NORAD (Shio et al 1994).

The rationale of RIDEPs was to support multifaceted development, on the assumption that the 'trickle down' effect was an inefficient vehicle for distributing economic growth to the poor (Shio et al 1994). However, by the early 1980s practitioners of integrated approaches particularly in Africa came to realise that RIDEPSs were also not a panacea. On the contrary, they appeared to impose strains on developing countries by their excessive demands on multi-ministry coordination. Due to these problems, the rate of donor dropout was so great that by 1986 only three regions were still operating integrated programmes with donor support, namely Iringa, Tanga and Kilimanjaro regions (Ngasongwa 1988).

Another reason for the poor success of RIDEPs was the fact that there was no vertical integration to ensure grassroots participation from the lower organs of the administrative structure that would have enabled them to interact freely and mutually with the target group in project implementation. They had to work through project officers as intermediaries and this lengthened the bureaucratic line, a fact that negates the good elements of an integrated plan.

Horizontal integration was also weak. Given the limited expertise in the regions the programmes did not have enough personnel to implement them in a holistic way that involved all the sector departments at a time.

The Tanzanian political system had dismantled the system of local government in the early 1970s. With the re-installation of local government in 1984, districts became the focal points of people's development administration and the regions were relegated to being coordinating organs of regional development. The results of these changes left RIDEPs exposed to pressures from local government and target groups, and programmes changed from a regional to a district focus.

Between economic crises

Despite the fact that there had been a reduction in productivity in some sectors, Tanzania registered substantial growth in a number of sectors in the late 1960s and early 1970s. The growth was attained in food security, income, education and health services. However, from the mid-1970s, a series of natural, internal and external events disrupted the economic growth trend. These events included a drought in 1973–74, the oil crisis in 1973, more droughts in 1974–75, the breaking up of the East African Community in 1977 and the war between Tanzania and Uganda in 1979.

At a global level, while a number of countries such as the Nordic ones had showered Nyerere's government with unconditional economic assistance, the ideologies of the economic superpowers turned against countries such as Tanzania from the late 1970s and early 1980s. The ideologies of Thatcherism (Margaret Thatcher was elected prime minister of the United Kingdom in 1979) and Reaganism (Ronald Reagan was elected president of United State of America in 1981) called for the reduction of the role of government and established conservative agendas (even though they left their own post-war welfare state programmes intact).

Faced with unprecedented economic woes arising from this conservative agenda, Tanzania tried home-grown economic recovery programmes such as the National Economic Survival Programme (NESP) between 1981 and 1983. Another economic policy Mwalimu Nyerere undertook before stepping down voluntarily from power in 1985 was the trade liberalisation of 1984.

Nyerere and the International Monetary Fund

Even though there are many things that Mwalimu Nyerere is remembered for at the global level, on the economic front, I think that it is the showdown with the International Monetary Fund

(IMF) which is the most relevant example. Bolstered by the conservative agenda, the international financial institutions (IFIs), particularly the World Bank and the IMF, veered away from their initial objectives and decided to advance the liberalise, marketise and privatise (LIMP) agenda to developing countries. With keener foresight than the majority of leaders, Mwalimu questioned 'Who made the IMF the International Ministry of Finance?'

Tanzanians of all persuasions, including myself, as a schoolboy in 1981, were organised to march against the IMF's conditionalities countrywide. Even though Nyerere's dissident voice was not properly heard due to the cacophony generated by proponents of market fundamentalism, recent events in the world economic system have put the IMF in the spotlight once again. When the IMF failed to provide a candid solution to the Far East (Asian) financial crises in the late 1990s, pundits questioned the efficacy of such a body. Similarly, in the current financial crisis, caused by a thicket of insurance scams, sub-prime bubbles and derivative trading in the major economies, which climaxed in September 2008, the same old question about the efficacy of the IMF has been raised once again.

It can be concluded that after trying the LIMP and similar approaches commonly undertaken under the Washington consensus banner in many developing countries with little results, the IFIs now seem to have shrewdly toned it down. Way back in 1998 Mwalimu Nyerere questioned the efficacy of the IFIs' agendas and dispositions. In his interview with Ikaweba Bunting on that year he contrasted the pre- and post-structural adjustment eras:

> I was in Washington last year. At the World Bank the first question they asked me was 'how did you fail?' I responded that we took over a country with 85 per cent of its adult population illiterate. The British ruled us for 43 years. When they left, there were 2 trained engineers and 12 doctors. This is the country we inherited.
>
> When I stepped down there was 91-per-cent literacy and nearly every child was in school. We trained thousands of engineers and doctors and teachers.
>
> In 1988 Tanzania's per-capita income was $280. Now, in 1998, it is $140. So I asked the World Bank people what went wrong. Because for the last ten years Tanzania has been signing on the

dotted line and doing everything the IMF and the World Bank wanted. Enrolment in school has plummeted to 63 per cent and conditions in health and other social services have deteriorated. I asked them again: 'what went wrong?' These people just sat there looking at me. Then they asked what could they do? I told them have some humility. Humility – they are so arrogant!

(Bunting 1999)

Fast forward to the current situation

I want to end this chapter by briefly revisiting the world's current economic situation. After the fall of the Berlin Wall in 1989, it seemed to a number of people that western liberalism had gained a universal triumph that meant that they could declare the 'end of history.' However, the current financial meltdown has just proved how right those were who never ceased to question the sustainability of a capitalist system that continued to be hinged on 'irrational exuberance', greed and weak regulatory systems.

However, to a significant extent, the capitalist system (at least in the West) is relatively more responsive to realities on the ground. For example, we are witnessing how, after they had realised the fault lines in unregulated market capitalism, the western economies are embracing the major tenets of socialist policies. Examples of such policies include types of nationalisation of critical economic systems such as financial institutions (at least for a while) or pouring in a massive amount of public funds to ensure the institutions work, provision of generous welfare benefits, and nationalisation of healthcare.

This chapter has pinpointed a number of economic policies under Mwalimu Nyerere which were deployed to bring socioeconomic development to Tanzanians. These policies had mixed results. While a number of indicators on the HDI improved appreciably, productivity in some sectors did not do so, resulting in a decline in economic growth. Due to a number of factors, including the absence of quick policy responses to economic feedback such as the declining economic growth, the Tanzanian economy took a long period to recover.

Nevertheless, the underlying philosophy of Nyerere's economic policies of building an egalitarian society has enabled

Tanzania to attain the status of a stable nation. A key lesson from Nyerere's economic policies is that in order to deliver desirable socio-economic development and stability to the citizens, economic policies must aim at increasing productivity in all sectors while also being egalitarian. This is because it is indisputable that no nation has ever developed without increasing productivity. Equally, sustainable egalitarian distribution of national wealth can be attained if there is sufficient economic growth wrought by increased productivity.

References

Bunting, I. (1999) 'The heart of Africa: interview with Julius Nyerere on anti-colonialism', *New Internationalist*, no. 309, http://www.hartford-hwp.com/archives/30/049.html, accessed 10 December 2009

Ellman, A. (1975) 'Development of Ujamaa policy in Tanzania', in L. Cliffe and P. Lawrence (eds), *Rural Cooperation in Tanzania*, Dar es Salaam, Tanzania Publishing House

Government of Tanganyika (1964) *Tanganyika Five-Year Plan for Economic and Social Development 1st July, 1964/65–30th June, 1969*, Dar es Salaam, Government Printer

Kamuzora, F. (2002) 'An evaluation of rural development during Mwalimu Nyerere's government using sustainable livelihood approach', *Uongozi Journal of Management Development* (Nyerere Special Edition), pp. 76–98

Ngasongwa, J. (1988) 'Foreign-assisted regional integrated development projects in Tanzania (1972-1987)', conference paper, Development and Project Planning Centre, University of Bradford

Nyerere, J.K. (1968) *Ujamaa: Essays on Socialism*, Oxford, Oxford University Press

Shio, L. et al (1994) 'Rural development strategies in Tanzania: the case of Rukwa Development Programme', Agder College – Institute of Development Management Collaboration Research Report, no. 3

Woods, R. (1975) 'Peasants and peasantry in Tanzania and their role in socio-political development', in L. Cliffe and P. Lawrence (eds), *Rural Cooperation in Tanzania*, Dar es Salaam, Tanzania Publishing House

Mwalimu Nyerere's ideas on land

Ng'wanza Kamata

Mwalimu Nyerere's thoughts on land can be understood at two levels. The first is his perception of land based on African traditions. The second is his belief that land is the basis of development, but equally, if not checked, the basis of differentiation, inequality and consequently political instability, especially in poor and underdeveloped societies such as Tanzania. It is around these two levels of perception that I explore and discuss Nyerere's thoughts on land.

Land is a free gift from God

Nyerere's views on land begin with his rejection of land as a commodity because such land cannot, under any circumstances, be transformed into an item for sale in the market. A related view is that land cannot be privately owned, i.e. land cannot be private property. The first time his views were articulated comprehensively was, perhaps, in 1958 when he published a pamphlet entitled *Mali ya Taifa* (*National Property*), which was a comment on the colonial government's proposal for new legislation regarding land holding. In this pamphlet he discarded any ideas which attempted to commodify or privatise land. The basis for his position was his belief that land, like water and air, is the gift of God to his living creation. Humans do not create or add to land, they are born to find it there and die to leave it there.

> All human beings, be they children brought up in poor or rich families, or belonging to sinners or saints, or even those whose parents are either slaves or free men, were born to find land in

existence. They can neither add to it or reduce its extent. It is God's gift, given to all His creation without any discrimination.

(Nyerere 1974, p. 53)

Nyerere underscores this point later on in his *Ujamaa – The Basis of Socialism*. Here he argued that 'we don't need to take degrees in Economics to know that neither the worker nor the landlord produces land. Land is God's gift to man – it is always there' (Nyerere 1977, p. 4).

One observation can be made about Nyerere's world view on land. First, his views are in many ways similar to those of Karl Polanyi on what he calls fictitious commodities. Polanyi differentiates between real and fictitious commodities. For him, a commodity is something that has been produced for sale on a market. By this definition, land, labour and money are fictitious commodities because they were not originally produced to be sold on a market (Polanyi 2001, p. xxv). But Nyerere, unlike Polanyi, misses the point that under certain conditions of production systems both land and labour may be transformed into commodities. The commoditisation of labour, land, and money, Polanyi explains, is a result of 'the development of a factory system' (Polanyi 2001, p. 79) which is organised 'as part of a process of buying and selling'. He further notes that:

[L]abour, land, and money had to be transformed into commodities in order to keep production going. They could, of course, not be really transformed into commodities, as actually they were not produced for sale on the market. But the fiction of their being so produced became the organising principle of society.

(Polanyi 2001, p. 79)

It is important here to note that for labour what is actually transformed into commodity is labour power, not labour; and for land to be transformed into capital, it must first be transformed into commodity. The process that transforms both labour and land into commodities begins, as Karl Marx noted, with the complete separation of the labourer from the means of production. Marx wrote:

The capitalist system pre-supposes the complete separation of the labourers from all property in the means by which they can realise their labour. As soon as capitalist production is once in its own legs, it not only maintains this separation, but reproduces it on a continually extending scale. The process, therefore, that clears the way for the capitalist system, can be none other than the process which takes away from the labourers the possession of his means of production; a process that transforms, on the one hand, the social means of substance and production into capital, on the other, the immediate producers into wage-labourers.

(Marx 1981, p. 668)

The process Marx is talking about began during a period he refers to as that of the primitive accumulation of capital. But under the neoliberal era even money itself becomes a commodity, as Polanyi alludes to. Originally, money (M) in the possession of a capitalist would be used to buy capital goods (C) and at the end of a cycle of production process the capitalist would have earned more money than originally invested (M1), hence the Marxist formulation of M - C - M1 where M1 is greater than M. Under neoliberalism, because of the shift from the economics of production to the economics of speculation, money buys money and hence the formulation M - M - M1. This has been part of the gambling (casino capitalism) economics dominating neoliberal economic practices.

On the basis of the foregoing observation, Nyerere is right that by its nature, land is not a commodity. But this can only be true under certain conditions and systems of production and distribution of wealth in society. It cannot be true in all conditions and systems of production. 'Just as labour, by nature, is not a commodity', writes Issa Shivji, 'so land, by nature, is not capital' (Shivji 2006, p. 8). Under capitalism both land and labour become commodity and capital respectively. The conditions under which land becomes capital include the establishment of 'a monopoly of access to land called ownership' and negotiability (Shivji 2006).

There is a point at which Nyerere seems to understand the conditions upon which land may become a commodity. His understanding, however, is a bit ambiguous. It is first considered alien to Africa, introduced by the colonialists, and secondly, it is a 'capitalist attitude ... foreigners introduced – the concept of land as a marketable commodity' (Nyerere 1977, p. 7). Here Nyerere is completely oblivious to the dialectical connection between colonialism and capitalism. It is correct that the system of land

107

tenure the colonial government wanted to promote was alien to a non-capitalist society which, as Walter Rodney would say, was following an independent path of development. But obviously the system was not alien to capitalism and its imperial interests in the colonies. It was thus not just an attitude of mind of capitalism, as Nyerere tries to suggest, but a historical outcome of the process which brought into being private property, commodification, and expropriation of the masses within the capitalist countries and overseas.

As a result of this lack of understanding, Nyerere's rejection of the idea of land as a commodity was based on its moral appeal. And as Fred Block says, such moral appeal suggests that 'it is simply wrong to treat nature (land) and human beings (labour) as objects whose price will be determined entirely by the market. Such a concept violates the principles that have governed societies for centuries' (quoted in Polanyi 2001, p. xxv). The basis of Nyerere's morality is African traditional life, which in itself would not prevent capital transforming land into a commodity and private property.

Land cannot be privately owned

Apart from the moral appeal Nyerere had other concerns regarding the privatisation of land. This was with respect to what would happen in Tanganyika if land were to be made private property. On this he said:

> [I]f people are given land to use as their property, then they have the right to sell it. It will not be difficult to predict who, in fifty years time, will be the landlords and who the tenants. In a country such as this, where, generally speaking, the African are poor and the foreigners are rich, it is quite possible that, within eighty or a hundred years, if the poor African were allowed to sell his land, all the land in Tanganyika would belong to wealthy immigrants, and the local people would be tenants. But even if there were no rich foreigners in this country, there would emerge rich and clever Tanganyikans. If we allow land to be sold like a robe, within a short period there would only be a few Africans possessing land in Tanganyika and all the others would be tenants.

(Nyerere 1974, p. 55)

Nyerere's fear of having all land alienated to non-natives was expressed as early as 1955, at the 15th session of the Trusteeship Council of the United Nations. He said:

> We shall also welcome immigrants who come to our country for the purpose of setting up specific industries or for doing business with us ... *But we are opposed to the farmer class of immigrant, which is largely European, and the general class of immigrant, which is largely from Asian ... Vast tracts of land have been alienated to non-Africans* [emphasis added]. We have never advocated that those non-Africans should be deprived of this land. But we have insisted that the period of ninety-nine-year leases is too long; that in those ninety-nine years the population of the country will have more than trebled itself; and that therefore leases ought, from the very beginning, to have been granted for shorter periods of thirty-three years; and that before being renewed the needs of the indigenous people should be considered first.
>
> (Nyerere 1974, p. 38)

There is no doubt that land was being alienated in Tanganyika during that time. One classical example that Nyerere referred to in passing just after his statement above is that of the famous Meru land case. The report of the Presidential Commission of Inquiry into Land Matters shows that some 2.3 million acres were alienated between 1949 and 1957 (URT 1994, p. 15). This was done under the powers vested in the colonial governor who, under the Land Ordinance of 1923, was 'empowered to dispose of land either to a native or a non-native ... In practice, this power was used almost exclusively to alienate land to non-natives' (URT 1994, p. 13). If this were to continue unchecked (and this, according to the proposal, was later to be converted into freehold), it was obvious who would be the landlord and who the tenant.

Nyerere's opposition to land as private property was also based on two other considerations. The first was the possibility of social differentiation, class contradictions, conflicts and bloodshed. He was troubled by the fact that freehold would cause the emergence of 'a small group of landlords and a large group of tenants'. This would create 'antagonism among peoples' (Nyerere 1974, p. 56). He drew on experiences from other countries where such developments caused violent conflicts. The most recent experience is the Zimbabwe land question and reform process and the classical one is the Mau Mau struggles for land in Kenya in the 1950s. In this regard Nyerere is right and his ideas echoes those of Polanyi and others before and after him who believed that commodification of fictitious property would be resisted.

The second consideration was exploitation. In a society like Tanzania, which he deemed to be classless, and where he envisioned building a socialism based on African traditions that was a non-exploitative society, private ownership of land would defeat this goal. In a freehold system, he lamented, 'We will get a group of people working to fulfil God's law of earning one's living through one's own labour. But there will be another group of idle people who will not be doing any work but will simply be waiting to exploit the energies, and suck the blood of the poor workers. And these bloodsuckers will not even allow the poor workers to earn fair wages for their labour' (Nyerere 1974, p. 56). This is a class that exploits because it owns land, and in the Arusha Declaration nomenclature this is the class of the *makabaila* (landlords).

He also feared that the freehold system would create a parasite class, a class surviving on speculation on land markets. To him these 'exploiters will rob the workers of everything they raise from their labours by charging exorbitant land rents, leaving them only what is barely adequate for a hand-to-mouth existence, and for keeping them fit to continue serving the masters' and one 'group will therefore reap what it did not plant, and the other group will plant but will not reap anything' (Nyerere 1974, p. 56). The logic behind his opposition to this speculative practice is succinctly captured in the following illustration:

> I could take a few square miles of land, call them 'mine' and then go off to the moon. All I had to do to gain a living from 'my' land was to charge a rent to the people who wanted to use it. If this piece of land was in an urban area I had no need to develop it at all; I could leave it to the fools who were prepared to develop all the other pieces of land surrounding 'my' piece, and in doing so automatically to raise the market value of mine. Then I could come down from the moon and demand that these fools pay me through their noses for the high value of 'my' land – a value which they themselves had created for me while I was enjoying myself on the moon!
>
> (Nyerere 1977, p. 7)

The consequences of privatisation or of letting loose private interests on land, are indisputable. Ten years after his death land disputes and cases of displacement of masses of people are common in Tanzania. This is a logical consequence of liberalism. One could, however, argue that even under his rule this happened. The case of Basuto and Mulbadaw villages in Hanang districts versus the then National Agricultural and Food Cooperation (NAFCO) attests to what happened. However, the difference is that land under Ujamaa was acquired for what were regarded as 'state' farms, and today, it is 'grabbed' for private interests, particularly a group known as '*wawekezaji*' (investors).

Moreover, what is happening today has its roots in the colonial past. Much as Nyerere was opposed to privatisation, and believed that land should be controlled by the people, he embraced the colonial Land Ordinance of 1923 unchanged. The ordinance 'statised' land in Tanzania, and established the basic principle of land tenure. These were not changed even after the 1999 land laws reforms. It would appear that Nyerere's major problem with the colonial system was freehold, and not that the ordinance vested land in the state, which was an alien state. He seems to have believed that once freehold was abolished, as was done in 1962, and leasehold introduced, and once the state was no longer alien, land would remain under the control of the people. On this he was wrong, as government bureaucrats replaced the people, and the laws, such as the Land Acquisition Act of 1967, allowed it. This is the way they were and are able to evict people from their lands.

Resisting private interest in land

What then should be done to prevent privatisation and commoditisation of land? In his thoughts Nyerere ascribed special roles to people's government, the people themselves, and the establishment of leasehold instead of freehold.

Throughout history people have resisted expropriation of their lands and other rights to resources. People have fought wars, and excessive forces have been used to evict the masses from their means of production. This was rampant in colonial Tanganyika. But it was evident that alienation did not go down well with the people as the Meru case exemplified. In the 1950s Nyerere was arguing that the Meru land should be returned. He stated:

> But there is one case of already-alienated land where nothing can satisfy my people except the complete return of the land to the people concerned. I mean the Meru land. I realise the delicacy of this matter, and therefore I do not intend to dwell upon it. I only want to emphasise that we are opposed to the purpose and the manner in which this land was alienated, and we hope that it shall be returned to the people concerned.
>
> (Nyerere 1974, p. 38)

In the 1970s Nyerere, as president of Tanzania, was faced with a more or less similar situation. The manner in which the land in Hanang was alienated was brutal and unjust. But his reaction to it was completely different from how he reacted to the Meru case. A witness to the Mulbadaw village case had this to say when they went to see Nyerere and other leaders:

> We complained to Government and party Leaders in Babati, Arusha, Dodoma and Dar es Salaam. We were not given any help. We were told *'poleni sana'* ... We said we had become like chicken – when the NAFCO farms are harvested we follow behind like chicken and pick up left over wheat. They told us that as the case was in Court we would be helped there. We met His Excellency the President himself. He said he did not want to make any decision as the matter was in Court.
>
> (Civil Case No. 10 of 1981)

The judgement for this case was delivered on 3 December 1984, a year before Nyerere stepped down as president. NAFCO appealed to the High Court and the judgement was delivered in June 1985, eight months after Ali Hassan Mwinyi became president. NAFCO won the case, and the claims of all the other plaintiffs failed. (Civil Appeal Case No. 3 of 1985). The land did not go back to the people, and even after the NAFCO project collapsed, the land was privatised.

When the land in Hanang was alienated the people resisted and Nyerere's government sent the police to evict them by force. Somewhere in his ideas he seems to suggest that people should not be ready to voluntarily accept enslavement. This in my view suggests that people need to – and should – resist. On refusing enslavement Nyerere wrote:

> When a lot of people accept the introduction of a method which will enable a few people to claim ownership of a thing which is actually God's gift to all His people, they are in actual fact, voluntarily accepting slavery. It is not necessary to be bought in order to be someone's slave. You can be a slave of whoever is able to rob you of the products of your labour on the pretext that you are using his land … any country which allows this practice by law is accepting voluntary slavery.
>
> (Nyerere 1974, p. 56)

The context of this statement was colonialism and the state was nakedly alien. Thus it was obvious and easy to convince the masses who would be the master and who the slave. But this could happen and might be happening now, when, of course, the state is not nakedly alien. Yet it is headed and run by citizens of a *comprador* class who might be leading their people and their countries into 'voluntary' enslavement. It would seem to me that Nyerere would be surprised if the masses would let this happen. The underlying clarion call in the quotation above is for the masses to resist and fight against this. This is despite the fact that he himself could withstand the masses' resistance.

The other solution to the freehold system was to put in place a leasehold system. Nyerere was of the view that this was the only way: to refuse to distribute land on a freehold basis as our forefathers did (Nyerere 1974, p. 56). Leasehold gives land to everybody who needs land. However, those given land do not own it but have a usufruct right to use it under certain conditions stated in the leasehold agreement, which lay down instructions to be followed by the person using and maintaining that land. This system, according to Nyerere, 'gives a person three things; sufficient land, security and a way of raising capital', meaning the leaseholder had the right to use land as security to raise a loan (Nyerere 1974, pp. 56 and 57). Land, though, remains the property of the public and a leaseholder would return the land to the public immediately they stopped using it. This way would also 'prevent greedy people from accumulating land for themselves without being able to use it' (Nyerere 1974, p. 57).

Nyerere, however, recognised the right of people to claim compensation for land which under certain circumstances had to be disposed of to the public for other use or users. The basis of this claim was, in his view, the labour invested in clearing and developing a piece of land. He argued that: 'when I use my energy and talent to clear a piece of ground for my use it is clear that I am trying to transform this basic gift from God so that it can satisfy a human need' (Nyerere 1974, p. 53). He elaborates this point further in the following way:

> But it is not really the land itself that belongs to me but only the cleared ground which will remain mine as long as I continue to work it. By clearing that ground I have actually added to its value and have enabled it to be used to satisfy a human need. Whoever then takes this piece of ground must pay me for adding value to it through clearing it by my own labour.
>
> (Nyerere 1974, p. 54)

A more solid view along these lines is that of Vandana Shiva, who dismisses the western conception of property, which respects only capital investment and not the fact that conception of non-western indigenous communities and cultures recognise that investment can also be of labour and nurturance (Shiva 2001, p. 44). Although Nyerere held this view, in practice his government acted to the contrary. Like the colonial state before him, more and more land, especially of the pastoralist communities, was alienated. This was based on the following:

> The misconception that pastoralists wander randomly gives rise to the belief that pastoral claims to particular land are fluid and temporary. This and the supposition that land not grazed at any one time is 'free', have resulted in the pastoralists losing a great deal of land without receiving compensation.
>
> (Lane 1998, p. 155)

Finally, Nyerere hoped that a government of the people would be the custodian of land on behalf of all, as discussed above. But one point that needs to be emphasised here is that as long as land continues to be controlled by the state (and its bureaucracy) the majority will be robbed of their lands. In no time the consequences Nyerere predicted some 51 years ago could happen. It has been suggested in Tanzania, and it is important to reiterate that suggestion, that land – especially that which belongs to the people – should be vested in the people. The people who depend on land live in village communities and the body which represents them all is the village assembly, so legally, village land should be vested in this organ.

Land and development

One of the immediate tasks of the independent government was development. After five years of a development path which relied heavily upon foreign aid and assistance, the government realised that it had to rethink and redefine its path to development and the means of achieving that. The attempt to do this came in 1967 in the form of the Arusha Declaration. The Arusha Declaration placed a lot of emphasis on land and thus agriculture as the route to development and defined development in terms of meeting the needs of the majority. The Arusha Declaration categorically stated that there are four prerequisite for development: people; land; good policies; and good leadership (Nyerere 1977, p. 29).

Why did Nyerere put a lot of emphasis on land? There were two reasons. The first was his abhorrence of the tendency, after independence, to rely heavily on money as the basis of development. The Arusha Declaration makes it clear that money was not the basis of development:

> [I]n the past we have chosen the wrong weapon for our struggle, because we chose money as our weapon. We are trying to overcome our economic weakness by using the weapon of the economically strong … by our thoughts, words and actions it appears as if we have come to the conclusion that without money we cannot bring about the revolution we are aiming at … It is as if we have said that 'money is the basis of development'.
>
> (Nyerere 1977, p. 18)

This tendency, however, did not go away completely with the pronouncement of the Arusha Declaration. Tanzania continued to receive increasing foreign aid after 1967. Mwesiga Baregu (1987, p. 3) shows that in 1967 Tanzania's dependency on foreign aid was nearly 26 per cent and it stood at nearly 70 per cent 10 years after the Arusha Declaration. This suggests that the 'question of aid dependency was never really quite resolved' (Baregu 1987, p. 5). The tendency has survived not only the Arusha Declaration but Nyerere himself, as the leadership which succeeded him shamelessly parade in front of foreign countries, proudly holding their leaking begging bowls.

The second reason why land was given a central place is that dependency on money, especially through foreign aid, would endanger the country's independence: if the country could not raise all the money it required for its development then it would have to seek foreign aid. This was wrong because, on the one hand, 'independence means self-reliance, that a country cannot really be independent if it depends on other nations for its development' (Nyerere 1977, p. 23), and on the other, 'even if we could get all that we need, such dependence upon others would endanger our independence and our ability to choose our own political policies' (Nyerere 1977, p. 25). There is no doubt about this, but it was not enough to speak out against the need for foreign aid without addressing and restructuring the dependent economy, a survivor of the colonial economy that was designed to serve imperial interests. It is partly because of the failure to address its structural dependency that Tanzania was brought to its knees by the World Bank and the IMF in the 1980s. The country was compelled to adopt structural adjustment programmes (SAPs) because the government could not survive without foreign aid.

To avoid the problems related to money, Nyerere saw the rural areas as providing the route to development, land being the basic means of doing this. He was convinced that this was possible because Tanzania had good land for producing a variety of crops for food and export, and for grazing cattle, goats and other stock (Nyerere 1977, p. 29).

His conception of development was centred on meeting the needs of the majority and here food came first. He also believed that all other needs could be realised if more efforts were placed on food production:

> And because the main aim of development is to get more food, and more money for our other needs, our purpose must be to increase production of these agricultural crops. This is in fact

the only road through which we can develop our country – in other words, only by increasing our production of these things can we get more food and more money for every Tanzanian.

(Nyerere 1977, p. 29)

This is another point he is introducing, and that is land-based production was the basis for capital accumulation. In other words, industrial development and development in other sectors would be based and dependent on the growth of agriculture. This point is further elaborated in the following statement:

Because the economy of Tanzania depends and will continue to depend on agriculture and animal husbandry, Tanzania can live well without depending on help from outside if they use their land properly. Land is the basis of human life and all Tanzanians should use it as a valuable investment for future development.

(Nyerere 1977, p. 33)

For 'future development', Nyerere meant industrialisation and 'modernity'. However, he envisaged some undesirable outcomes if 'national development' (industrialisation and modernity) depended on rural areas. This is what he described as 'exploitation' of the rural areas by the urban areas. This was based on his analysis that neither industrialisation nor foreign aid could be paid up by people other than those engaged in agriculture, the rural people. He was aware that if Tanzania was to industrialise, the capital would come from agriculture, and even if the money were a loan from external sources its repayment would not be made from 'urban and industrial development' but from the rural areas (Nyerere 1977, p. 27). To prevent this he discouraged industrialisation. His argument was that industrialisation should be an outcome of development not the means for development. The 'mistake we are making is to think that development begins with industries. It is a mistake because we do not have the means to establish many modern industries in our country. We do not have the necessary finances or the technical know-how' (Nyerere 1977, p. 26).

Conclusion

Nyerere held very strong views against land commoditisation and privatisation. This fitted in well with his vision for building Ujamaa – African socialism – in Tanzania. Unfortunately though, he did not manage to put in place mechanisms which would prevent the occurence of those things that he did not desire. There were many positive reforms on land which he made while in power, but these did not manage to transform the major issues whose legacy would have helped in ensuring that land was, and remained, under the control of the people. Out of power Nyerere looked back and reflected. The good thing is that he knew where he went wrong or did not do enough. In an interview with Ikaweba Bunting in 1998, Nyerere was asked: 'What were your main mistakes as Tanzanian leader? What should you have done differently?'

And his response, which concludes my discussion, was:

> There are things that I would have done more firmly or not at all. For example, I would not nationalise the sisal plantations. This was a mistake. I did not realise how difficult it would be for the state to manage agriculture. Agriculture is difficult to socialise. I tried to tell my government that what was traditionally the family's in the village social organisation should be left with the family, while what was new could be communalised at the village level. *The land issue and family holdings were very sensitive. I saw this intellectually but it was hard to translate it into policy implementation* [emphasis added]. But I still think that in the end Tanzania will return to the values and basic principles of the Arusha Declaration.
>
> (Bunting 1999)

References

Bunting, Ikaweba (1999) 'The Heart of Africa. Interview with Julius Nyerere on Anti-Colonialism', *New Internationalist*, no. 309, January–February

Baregu, Mwesiga (1987) 'The paradox of the Arusha Declaration', *The African Review*, vol. 14, nos 1 and 2

Civil Appeal No. 3 of 1985, National Agriculture and Food Corporation versus Mulbadaw Village Council and Others

Civil Case No. 10 of 1981, Mulbadaw Village Council and Others versus National Agriculture and Food Corporation

Lane, Charles R. (ed) (1998) *Custodian of the Commons*, London, Earthscan
  Publications
Marx, Karl (1981) *Capital*, Moscow, Progress Publishers
Nyerere, Julius, K. (1974) *Freedom and Unity*, Dar es Salaam and Addis
  Ababa, Oxford University Press
Nyerere, Julius, K. (1977) *Ujamaa: Essays on Socialism*, Dar es Salaam and
  Nairobi, Oxford University Press
Polanyi, Karl (2001) *The Great Transformation: The Political and Economic Origin
  of Our Time*, Boston, MA, Beacon Press
Shiva, Vandana (2001) *Protect or Plunder: Understanding Intellectual Property
  Rights*, London and New York, Zed Books
Shivji, Issa G. (2006) 'Lawyers in neoliberalism: authority's professional
  supplicants or society's amateurish conscience', valedictory lecture on the
  occasion of his formal retirement from the University of Dar es Salaam
United Republic of Tanzania (URT) (1994) *Report of the Presidential
  Commission of Inquiry into Land Matters*, Dar es Salaam and Uppsala,
  Sweden, Ministry of Land, Housing and Urban Development and The
  Scandinavia Institute of African Studies

The village in Mwalimu's thought and political practice

Issa G. Shivji

Village as a site of development

The village was dear to Mwalimu's heart but not in any romantic sense, as his western admirers would want to present it. 'Small-is-beautiful' or 'tradition-is-sacrosanct' were not part of Mwalimu's political practice, although one could find some isolated passages in his writings coming close to that. I want to suggest that Mwalimu's attitude to the village was very pragmatic. He saw Tanzania essentially as a nation of village communities and was likely to be so for the foreseeable future. Very often, he rationalised and justified villagisation as a means of accelerating development and facilitating the provision of health, education, water and other social services. But as is usually the case, the outcomes of history are not what the actors intended. In reality, the various villagisation programmes since independence became top–down centrist projects, allowing more intense exploitation and the siphoning off of surplus generated in the agrarian sector.

There are three broad phases in Mwalimu's attitude to and thoughts about the village. The basis of the first was the transformation approach recommended by the World Bank (Nyerere 1967, p. 183). This was the experiment in creating model farmers who would be settled in a village and provided with technology and managerial cadre. In his inaugural address as the first elected president of Tanganyika, Nyerere said that for the next few years his government would concentrate on bringing people together to live in villages. He continued:

And if you ask me why the Government wants us to live in villages, the answer is just as simple: unless we do we shall not be able to provide ourselves with the things we need to develop our land and to raise our standard of living. We shall not be able to use tractors; we shall not be able to provide schools for our children; we shall not be able to build hospitals, or have clean drinking water, it will be quite impossible to start small village industries, and instead we shall have to go on depending on the town for all our requirements; and even if we had a plentiful supply of electric power we should never be able to connect it up to each isolated homestead.

(Nyerere 1967, p. 184)

Mwalimu was adept at translating the advice of the 'experts', in this case the consultants of the World Bank who drew up the first three-year development plan, into a simple language and communicating it to his people. The heart of the World Bank villagisation programme was the modernisation theory which was rampant at the time. Traditional peasants had to be pulled into and integrated in the international commodity circuits. The programme was based on the so-called transformation and improvement approach. Model farmers would be settled in villages, given modern technology and they would farm under the supervision of managers. Others, outside the village settlement schemes, would learn from these model farmers by example. This model did not challenge the basic structures of the colonial economy, which was integrated vertically into metropolitan economies supplying raw materials while importing manufactured goods. Nor did it question the accumulation model at the heart of the colonial economy. This was based on the peasant as the reservoir of cheap labour who exerted super-human labour to enable plantation monopoly capital to reap super-profits.

For various reasons, the village settlement programme was a huge failure (Cliffe and Cunningham 1968). The relationship between the managers and the settlers was one of antagonism. Settler farmers had no motivation to work. Heavy machinery that had been bought with scarce foreign exchange could not be maintained and productively used. In any case, it was too expensive – since it was imported – to be affordable. The transformation and improvement approach was soon given up and village settlements abandoned. It is interesting to note that Mwalimu's rationalisation of the village settlement was based much more on the provision of basic social services than any economic model of development. While Nyerere had a broad vision of social development and while he was extremely articulate in communicating it *politically* to his people, he never understood the underlying political economy of a peripheral underdeveloped economy in the international capitalist system.

The next round of villagisation came after the Arusha Declaration of 1967 when the ruling party TANU and its government deliberately adopted the policy of socialism and self-reliance. While Mwalimu had talked about socialism – or Ujamaa – long before, it was always a kind of faith (*ujamaa ni imani*), rather than a political programme. The Arusha Declaration took a big leap forward. It explicitly referred to the incipient growth of classes in Tanzanian society and that if this were allowed to continue, the country would move away from its goal of creating a society of equals. It took concrete measures to forbid what it called exploitative tendencies by nationalising the commanding heights of the economy and prohibiting political leaders at the helm of the party and the state from indulging in private accumulation. Once again, its rural development model was based on small peasants coming together in villages to produce communally and share the fruits of their labour equally. This is what led to the creation of ujamaa villages.

But soon the government found that the small peasant was least interested in communal production. Ultimately, therefore, the government adopted the policy of 'development villages' and ordered peasants to live in them. This was called Operation Vijiji. Operation Vijiji has come to have negative connotations because movement into villages was no longer voluntary; it was forced and there was considerable use of paramilitary force to move some nine million people into villages within a period of four to five years.

There is no doubt that, while recognising some of the excesses of villagisation, Mwalimu considered villagisation as one of the important successes of the Arusha Declaration. In 'The Arusha Declaration ten years after', Mwalimu said:

In my Report to the 1973 TANU Conference I was able to say that 2,2028,164 people were living in villages. Two years later, in June, 1975, I reported to the next TANU Conference that approximately 9,100,000 people were living together in 7,684 villages. This is a tremendous achievement. It is an achievement of TANU and Government leaders in cooperation with the people of Tanzania. It means that something like 70 per cent of our people moved their homes in the space of about three years! All these people now have a new opportunity to organise themselves for local democratic government, and to work with the Regional, District, and Central administrations to hasten the provision of basic educational, health, and the other public services, which are necessary for a life in dignity. Results are already becoming apparent. Universal Primary Education by the end of 1977, for example, would have been out of the question had the people not been living in village communities by now. As it is, we stand a good chance of achieving that objective.

(Nyerere 1977, p. 65)

In many respects, Mwalimu's thought, and in particular his political practice, on the village complemented the conceptualisation of the village as a site of development, which I will discuss later. However, there are seeds of the conception of the village as a site of governance (such as, for example, the use of the phrase 'local democratic government' in the above quote) but these are fleeting references and, certainly, there is no evidence that he advocated any consistent, political programme to evolve village governance. The tendency of top–down state benevolence towards the peasant was strong in Mwalimu. No doubt he was sincere about it. His sincerity and personal devotion to uplifting the life of village communities accounts for the better standard of health, education, water, etc, in the villages during the period of the Arusha Declaration.

There is another interesting gap in Mwalimu's thought on the village. This is the virtual absence of his theorising village development as charting out a new path of development. In fact, there is an interesting consistency in Mwalimu's thought on one issue: he not only saw Tanzania as a country of village communities, he also wanted them to be virtually undifferentiated communities. In other words, his vision of the rural Tanzania was essentially that of a middle peasantry. His hostility to the rich peasant was

123

quite explicit. The Arusha Declaration, for example, describes the rich peasant as feudal (*kabaila*). We know that the rising rich peasantry in Ismani and Basotu, Hanang, was decimated. In the case of Ismani, the rich peasantry was ousted by force and ujamaa villages created in their place. There was considerable resistance resulting in the assassination of Dr Klerru by a rich peasant. Dr Klerru was the then regional commissioner of Iringa and a leading party cadre in the forefront of implementing rural socialism (*ujamaa vijijini*). The rich peasantry in Basotu, which was successfully growing wheat, were dispossessed and their land allocated to a giant parastatal company, the National Agriculture and Food Corporation (NAFCO). In that case the resistance of the peasants took the form of court cases, some of which remain unsettled to this day.

The Hanang wheat project under NAFCO was implemented with assistance from the Canadian International Development Association (CIDA), which also provided capital, machinery and the management. Ultimately, the project was a huge failure but meanwhile did considerable damage to the environment and the livelihoods of the peasantry. The NAFCO project ran counter to Nyerere's philosophy of rural socialism. Nyerere constantly emphasised the development of the small peasant and was known to be against big parastatal projects, yet NAFCO was precisely that.

Nyerere did not see NAFCO as a harbinger of capitalism, while the rich peasant was. Generally, Nyerere did not make a distinction between national capitalism and comprador capitalism[1] on the one hand, and private capitalism and state capitalism, on the other.

There were some very interesting shifts in Mwalimu's thought on the village after he stepped down from presidency. Unfortunately, these were not developed to the full, nor have they been the subject of much discussion. I can therefore cite only one speech and one personal anecdote to illustrate this shift and hope that intellectuals and researchers will revisit this period of Mwalimu's intellectual journey.

Some time around 1990, Mwalimu as a chair of the meeting of top government and parastatal executives, made an ex tempore closing speech. One part of that speech dwelt on an analysis of Ujamaa ideology as a legitimising ideology. I have dealt with this

elsewhere (Shivji 1995). For the present purpose, it is the other
section, which is profoundly interesting, that concerns us. I quote
the original Kiswahili (followed by my own non-literal translation
and interpolations):

*Kwa Coca-Cola kwa sababu Marekani wao wana nguvu sana kwa
Coca-Cola. Marekani sasa anataka wote tuwe ni wanywa Coca-Cola.*

*Ndugu Mengi[2] mkipenda msipende mtatuuzia tu Coca-Cola basi
Coca-Cola inauzwa tu. Sasa uchumi wetu basi ni uchumi tegemezi.
Uchumi wa nchi zetu hizi zote una sifa hizo mbili. Hili tatizo letu
kubwa la msingi. Uchumi wetu ni uchumi duni, lakini uduni peke yake
si kitu sana lakini tatizo kubwa kabisa kabisa ni uchumi tegemezi.*

*Kwa hiyo tunajivunia ule ugonjwa ... tuna jivunia ule ugonjwa
wala hatuuonei haya ... unaparedi silaha za wakubwa, unaparedi
madege ya wakubwa, unaparedi bidhaa za wakubwa, unaparedi
Macoca cola ya wakubwa na unajivunia tu unasema sisi tumeendelea.
Ukimwambia umeendelea kwanini, anakuwambia njoo uone barabara
yetu. ...*

*Tunao uchumi tunaweza kuuita wa kisasa, na uchumi wa kisasa
ni ule uchumi ulio chuma. Uchumi wa kisasa katika nchi hizi ni
wa kigeni. Kwa hiyo ni Coca-Cola chombo cha kigeni ni mtambo
unapokea tu pale ....*

*Eh! Yuko mhindi mmoja Kiswahili chake kilikuwa kizuri sana
kuliko cha Babu Patel. Aliniambia 'Mwalimu e wewe sema nak-
wishakata mirija lakini bomba je kwisha kata? Sasa mabomba ... sasa
uchumi wetu ule wa kisasa ni wa mabomba mwanzo wake huko nje.*

(Mzalendo, date misplaced)

[Americans are powerful and they want us to consume their
Coca-Cola; so we all drink Coca-Cola.

Brother Mengi,[2] whether you like it or not, you will continue
selling Coca-Cola to us. Our economy is basically a dependent
economy. The primary problem of our economy is its double
characteristic. One, it is weak, second, it is dependent. But
weakness in itself is not a big problem. The real problem is that
our economy is a dependent economy.

Nevertheless, we boast about this disease ... we do not even
feel ashamed of it. You parade the weapons of the superpowers, their planes, their commodities, their Coca-Colas, and still
boast that we have developed. When asked how are you developed, you respond, come and see our roads ...

We do have that economy which we can call a modern

economy ... modern economy is that which accumulates. But the modern economy in our countries is a foreign economy. And thus Coca-Cola is a foreign instrument [of accumulation?] ... you only receive the machinery [it is not yours] ...

Eh! There is this Indian – whose Kiswahili was better then Babu Patel's – he asked me: Mwalimu, you say you have cut the straws but what of the pumps ... have you cut the pumps? The problem is that our modern economy is one of these pumps which siphon off our wealth. And its origin lies outside.

In this, it seems to me, Mwalimu is distinguishing very graphically between a national capitalist and a comprador capitalist (or, what I later call, not quite exactly, 'accumulation from below' and 'accumulation from above').

The other, more relevant to our present discussion, is an anecdote. When we had completed our draft Land Commission Report (1994), the commissioners paid a visit to Mwalimu. This was sometime in 1991. I first explained to Mwalimu, in outline, the major recommendations of the commission. As I explain later, our recommendations on the reform of the land tenure system were based on the model of 'accumulation from below'. I don't know if that is how Mwalimu understood it. But I remember his reaction, which I can only paraphrase in translation, so these are not his exact words:

Yes, chairman [referring to Shivji], tell them [meaning the government] ... Tell them. I know, they won't listen. But tell them ... I have been telling them. Now you want 'commercial farmers' [in English] and you go to look for them in London.[3] Why? Who is a commercial farmer? For me a commercial farmer is that blessed fellow who cultivates his land with an oxen-plough, produces food for his family and sells the surplus on the market. We have such commercial farmers ... Look for them ... They are there; you don't have to go to London to find them...

I found this observation quite interesting, both in the light of what the Land Commission said it was going to recommend and Mwalimu's attitude to rich peasantry at the time of the Arusha Declaration. As I have already said, Mwalimu's earlier attitude to rich peasants was hostile while in this quote he is obviously advocating some form of rich peasant economy.

It is, however, the political or governance side of the villagisation process that I wish to reflect on in this chapter. This was least developed in Mwalimu's thought, yet, his political practice left behind important village institutions.

The village as a site of governance

During the period of the Arusha Declaration, the village was seen in mainstream conceptualisation and policymaking as a 'site of development', not as a site of governance. Villagers, therefore, were recipients of development which, translated into bureaucratic terms meant, receivers of directives, resolutions and orders from the top (*maagizo na maazimio*), not decision-makers, much less self-governing units. Development was supposed to be directed by directors of development – that is what they were called, DDDs (district development directors) and RDDs (regional development directors). Politically, villagers were supposed to be mobilised for development. The whole structure of governance was top–down, commandist, albeit politically populist.

As we know, the decentralisation programme of the early 1970s, which abolished local government and was planned and implemented at the behest of the American consultancy firm MacKinsey (Coulson 1982, p. 12), was a failure of no mean proportions. Decentralisation was in effect decentralisation of the central bureaucracy to lower levels. One of the dubious achievements of the decentralised bureaucracy was the implementation of the forced villagisation of the 1970s, Operation Vijiji. One of the decentralised civil servants linked decentralisation with Operation Vijiji. Explaining why the move was undertaken in 1973, a year after decentralisation, Juma Mwapachu said:

> The answer is linked to the TANU and government decision in June 1972 to overhaul the Governmental administrative structure. In particular, the regional administration was to move from its original law and order and revenue collection function into a more development-based management function with the people thoroughly involved at the grass-roots level in planning and implementation of development projects…
>
> Therefore, one year after the decentralisation programme was effected, TANU and Government saw the need to reinforce

the participatory development institution by creating a firmly
established, participating institution – planned villages.

(Mwapachu 1976, quoted in Coulson 1982, p. 116)

Populist rhetoric notwithstanding, there is substantial evidence
that villages were anything but participatory. Yet, a potentially
progressive institutional structure was created at the end of the villagisation period. The Villages and Ujamaa Villages (Registration,
Designation, and Administration) Act of 1975 created two important organs, the village assembly and an elected body, the village
council. When local government was reintroduced in 1982, these
two bodies were incorporated into the local government structure.
Thus villagisation established an irreversible structure, the village
structure. Some 15 years later, the Land Commission found that,
by and large, the village as established through villagisation was
accepted and had become part of the administrative structure,
albeit conceived by the state bureaucracy as being more on the
receiving end of central and local government machinery, rather
than the primary basis of democratic governance.

The conception and rhetoric of the donor-funded on-going
Local Government Reform Programme (LGRP), which was
launched in 1998, revolves around the efficient provision of social
services. Although it deploys the rhetoric of devolution of power,
transparency and accountability, the legal and institutional structure envisaged bears little relationship to the rhetoric. As a matter
of fact, typically, local government stops at the district level. In
bureaucratic outlook, the village is once again not a site of governance. If during the Arusha period it was the site of development,
under the LGRP it is the site of delivery of social services and
instead of political mobilisation, we have the apparently apolitical
awareness raising and capacity building of 'ignorant' peasants by
partners, meaning erstwhile NGOs and the so-called 'development practitioners'.

Summing up positive achievements

The wisdom of hindsight, I believe, allows us to better identify
certain positive and potentially progressive outcomes of the process of villagisation during the Arusha period.

First, the ideological context of the process was Ujamaa, a

vision of constructing a society based on human equality and dignity. Such a vision integrated Tanzanian society in the larger human project of social emancipation, on the one hand, and provided a collective perspective on global and local contestations of power and wealth, on the other. This stands in sharp contrast to the current ambitions to become part of a globalised world, no matter if our humanity, equality and dignity are sacrificed in the process.

Second, the process was firmly rooted in a developmentalist discourse. However economistic it became at times, it could not easily be reduced to empiricism. It created a terrain to raise and interrogate larger and broader trends in society and the direction of its movement. Nothing of this level of discourse is possible, or even attempted, within the current policy-dialogue, to use the obtuse jargon of modern-day consultants of 'poverty reduction'. Any one who has attended one of those 'stakeholder workshops' knows the amount of intellectual and material energy foolishly spent on identifying, quantifying, tabulating, etc, the most vulnerable and the poorest among the poor for the purposes of being 'targeted' for 'poverty alleviation'.

Third, the populist rhetoric of mass mobilisation had, of necessity, to be located on a political terrain and, therefore, inevitably brought in the contestation of power between vested interests in support of the status quo, on the one hand, and agencies of change, on the other. The current neoliberal discourse in the language of stakeholders, rapid rural appraisals, awareness creating, capacity building, and all that, pretends to be politically free 'dialogue' and 'consultation' among, ostensibly, equal 'partners' and 'stake-holders'!

Fourth, institutionally, the village assembly and the elected village council, have great potential as a site of democratic governance enabling organic contestations within village communities. This is the potential which was ironically suppressed by the developmentalist and populist rhetoric of the Ujamaa period.

As will be recalled, the Land Commission (1994) pegged its recommendations on land tenure reform around these organs and, in particular, its recommendation that village land be vested in the village assembly. I believe the land tenure structure woven around village organs demonstrates the interesting and progressive potential in the village assembly to create a whole new vision and terrain of political and economic contestation under the present circumstances. In the next section, I briefly summarise how the reform of village governance, as part of the local government reform programme, could be structured around village organs.

In a study done with a colleague on 'village democracy', we placed the restructuring of village governance centre stage. Our argument, firstly, proceeded from the conceptual shift in the village as a site of development or delivery of social services to the village as a site of governance.

Second, we argued, as a site of governance, the village constitutes the primary level or the third-tier governance structure, the other two being the district and the national. It is at these three levels only that the elected organs of the people with legislative and executive powers and functions are to be found. In bureaucratic, and even popular, consciousness and practice the region, which is only the site of administration, not governance, has greater weight and power in relation to the district. Similarly, the ward (for example, the ward development committee), which is a coordinating level of administration, is more powerful than the village government, which is an elected body.

Third, we argued that the relationship between different tiers of governance should be based on law and not administrative fiat. Thus the jurisdictions of district council and village council should be clearly demarcated in law.

Fourth, village governance should be based on the rule of law and the separation of power. Thus the venerable constitutional principles are applied at the village level with the village assembly as a legislative body and the village council as an executive body.

I have no doubt in my mind that some reform of this kind, in which the village is the centre of political governance, would have fitted well in Mwalimu's philosophy and political practice.

The political economy of village governance reform

What is the basis in political economy of the village governance reform we are advocating? In other words, what development trajectory is envisaged by this reform? In this paper, I cannot go into great details but would like to suggest tentatively the following theses for further investigation and reflection.

First, Tanzania is and will continue to be in the foreseeable future a country of smallholder peasant and pastoral production. It is the agrarian and pastoral sector which will continue to provide the surplus and which constitutes the potential source of accumulation.

Second, the feasible and sustainable path of development for the country is towards an integrated national economy producing largely for the national market. The key link in developing the economy in that direction is the agrarian (including pastoral) sector and within this the key link is the production of food for the national market and possible export of the surplus.

In other words, what needs to be done is to create enabling conditions for not only production of surplus in the agrarian sector but accumulation in that sector. This is what I call 'accumulation from below'. The colonial and post-colonial policies, including the current liberalised ones, have been based on accumulation from above. This means that although the agrarian sector generates surplus, this is siphoned off through various mechanisms and agencies, chiefly some form or other of merchant capital (whether the state, as under the Arusha Declaration, or private, as under liberalisation). Under the so-called liberalised/globalised economy and new land tenure system, there is a trend towards a new form of 'primitive accumulation', that is, the pillaging of natural resources, including genetic resources, mainly by foreign, including in our case South African, capital. This trend, in my view, is already happening and is groping for a stable political expression. One of the major effects of accumulation from above or merchant capital on the village community is to suppress and pervert internal differentiation.

Third, the purpose of the governance suggested here is to create enabling political conditions for internal differentiation and to ward off predatory outside capital. Of course, this assumes complementary reforms in other sectors, including the state itself. But it is suggested that the key link in the restructuring of the state is the village.

An interesting question that arises is about the social – class – character of such a state. Space does not allow us to go into the details of this. Suffice to say that what is envisaged is some kind of a national democratic state based on working people.

Mwalimu's thought did not capture the political economy aspect of his central emphasis on the village. I would dare suggest that this is because Mwalimu, unlike, for example, Nkrumah, did not fully understand or appreciate the political economy of imperialism. As is well known, he never accepted that building socialism was a process of class struggle. He did not therefore accept that the state he was the leader of had a class character. He believed that the state could carry out the reforms he genuinely believed in so long as it had a selfless, committed leadership.

Notes

1. Comprador capitalism refers to the local ruling class adopting the same basic economic system left behind by colonialism as opposed to transforming it into a national system answering to the needs of the large majority of producers.
2. A leading local entrepreneur who holds the Coca-Cola franchise.
3. At the time the then prime minister was holding a meeting with investors in London.

Bibliography

Coulson, A. (1982) *Tanzania: A Political Economy*, Oxford, Oxford University Press

Cliffe, L. and Cunningham, G.L. (1968) 'Ideology, organisation and the settlement experience in Tanzania', in Cliffe, L. and Saul, J. (eds) (1973) *Socialism in Tanzania: an Interdisciplinary Reader*, Nairobi, East African Publishing House

Land Commission, United Republic of Tanzania (1994) *Report of the Commission of Inquiry into Land Matters* (Shivji Commission), Dar es Salaam and Uppsala, Ministry of Lands, Housing and Urban Development and Scandinavian Institute of African Studies

Nyerere, J. (1967) *Freedom and Unity*, Oxford, Oxford University Press

Nyerere, J. (1977) 'The Arusha Declaration ten years after,' reprinted in Coulson, A. (ed) (1979) *African Socialism in Practice: The Tanzanian Experience*, Nottingham, Spokesman, pp. 43–74

Shivji, I.G. (1995) 'The rule of law and Ujamaa in the ideological formation of Tanzania', *Social and Legal Studies*, vol. 4, no. 2, pp. 147–74

Shivji, I.G. (2009) *Accumulation in an African Periphery: A Theoretical Framework*, Dar es Salaam, Mkuki na Nyota

Shivji, I.G. (2009) *Where is Uhuru?: Reflections on the Struggle for Democracy in Africa*, Oxford and Nairobi, Fahamu Books

Shivji, I.G. and Peter, C.M. (2000) *The Village Democracy Initiative: A Review of the Legal and Institutional Framework of Governance at Sub-district Level in the Context of Local Government Reform*, UNDP

Racial and religious tolerance in Nyerere's political thought and practice

Salma Maoulidi

What does racial and religious tolerance signify to a nation like Tanzania? Is it solely the absence of violent conflicts – *'kisiwa cha amani'* (an 'island or pocket of peace') – as described by the current 'political speak', or is it the absence of grievances explained as peaceful coexistence? Specifically, what is the legacy of Mwalimu Nyerere with regard to the question of racial and religious tolerance in the larger political culture of Tanzania?

The literature reviewed for this piece suggests strongly that the question of racial and religious tolerance has been glossed over. The fuzziness with which the matter has been dealt by successive governments can be summed up as a procrastinator's escapism, one promising a sure recipe for latent divisions and sowing a politics of hatred. Part of the myopia lies in the narrow scope within which the questions of race and religion are tackled by different writers. Equally problematic is the timidity with which commentators have taken up Mwalimu's response to religious and racial challenges.

Building on Nyerere's performance in this realm, I investigate the legacy left by Mwalimu to a young nation with respect to confronting racial and religious challenges. How did Mwalimu's personal values and beliefs influence his political agenda and trajectory? How far did his preoccupation with a racial or religious agenda contribute to fostering national unity and promoting a national agenda?

Race, racialism and representation

Nyerere is credited for a level of racial tolerance in Tanzania not witnessed in other countries in the region (Malambugi 2007; Ssekitooleko 2008; MacDonald 1966). His politics of moderation and racial harmony ensured that the African majority lived in relative peace with minorities in the territory. A disposition of racial harmony is, however, deeply rooted in the history/herstory of the vanguard of the independence struggle, the Tanganyika African National Union (TANU). Its rallying motto was *Uhuru na Umoja* ('Freedom and unity'). Rather than encourage racialism, TANU promoted nationalism, seeing people first and foremost as Tanganyikans.

Yet in both Tanganyika and Zanzibar, at the heart of the liberation struggle was the question of race. Therefore, the integrationist racial politics in TANU did not always find wide support among its adherents, leading to fissures among the leadership and membership. Zuberi Mtemvu, formerly the TANU secretary in the eastern province, for example, did not approve of TANU's racial politics. On this account he broke away and formed the African National Congress (ANC), a party constituted on a racial platform. The party's rallying slogan was 'Africa for Africans'. Another prominent party at the time, the United Tanganyika Party (UTP) – dubbed 'the governor's party' – advocated a representative system based on multiracialism (MacDonald 1966).

TANU membership was open to all ethnicities and races and as a party of moderate racial politics, the TANU 1954 constitution stressed peace, equality and racial harmony, while opposing tribalism, isolationism and discrimination. TANU members were urged to fight the racialist habits of thought – a colonial heritage. During the 1958 elections, TANU presented European as well as Asian candidates in different constituencies: Lady Chesham, a European, represented the Wahehe in the southern constituency of Iringa, while Sophia Mustafa, an Asian, ran for the northern constituency in Arusha.

This was later followed by Celia Paes, a Goan from Dar es Salaam and formerly the president of the Tanganyika Council of Women, and Barbro Johansson, a European who stood for a seat in Mwanza. Together with three African women, these women formed the cream of Tanganyika's elected and nominated representatives at independence. Their achievements were eclipsed by prominent non-African figures in the first cabinet, some of whom became close friends of Nyerere such as Amir Jamal, Al-Noor Kassam and Derek Bryceson.

Indoctrinating racial equality

To Nyerere, a self-proclaimed African socialist, socialism and racialism were incompatible. The basis of socialism is a belief in human equality. Socialism is not for the benefit of black men, nor brown men, nor white men, nor yellow men. The purpose of socialism is the service of man (read: humankind), regardless of colour, size, shape, skill, ability or anything else.

The Arusha Declaration of 1967, then the blueprint for African socialism (*Ujamaa*) in Tanzania, does not talk about racial groups or nationalities. It defines as friends those who stand for the interests of the workers and peasants, anywhere in the world. It urges against putting people in pre-arranged categories of race or national origin. Rather, it wants each individual judged according to her or his character and ability, similar to Martin Luther King Jr's plea for people to be judged by the content of their character.

Of course, there was an evolution in arriving at this point in both the TANU party and in the mind of its leaders. In his formative political career, Nyerere felt bitter about the favours which the Europeans enjoyed. He wanted to fight against discrimination, for African rights, for equal work and equal salaries. He later described these demands as the 'politics of sheer complaint', politics limited by his worldview at the time (*Africa News Online* 1999). As he became more exposed to politics and other races, he attained the sophistication of tolerating mutual coexistence and acknowledging the humanity of others in lieu of settling scores, all of which informed a more encompassing political strategy.

Examples cited where Nyerere demonstrated a politics of racial moderation include the April 1959 meeting of the Pan-African Freedom Movement of Eastern and Central Africa (PAFMECA) held in Zanzibar, where he was instrumental in bringing the Arab and African parties closer together as they struggled with ideological and racial divisions at the height of the independence struggle. Also during a PAFMECA meeting in Nairobi, Kenya, in September 1959, Nyerere diffused racial tensions by declaring that Europeans and Asians were welcome to remain in Africa as equal citizens after independence was achieved.

Anti-racial politics were prominent not only in the party's local agenda but also in its international agenda. On 26 June 1959 Julius Nyerere, along with Father Trevor Huddleston, at a meeting in London launched the 'Boycott South Africa movement', re-named in 1960 as the 'Anti-apartheid movement'. During the Commonwealth Prime Minister's Conference in London in March 1961, Nyerere joined other African leaders in denouncing the racist policies of the Union of South Africa. He threatened to boycott the body if South Africa remained in the Commonwealth, a threat that persuaded South Africa to withdraw its membership from the body. His anti-apartheid stance would go on to inform the creation of the Frontline States in which Tanzania played a prominent part, an initiative conceived to defeat racism and apartheid by containing it and confronting it both at home and abroad (Boddy-Evans).

Unlocking racialised political discourses

But despite all these efforts, prevailing racial tensions found expression immediately after independence. In Dar es Salaam, rioting, looting, rape and racial killings ensued as the mutineers took over the capital in 1964. British officers and non-commissioned officers (NCOs) were rounded up and expelled. The consequences in Zanzibar during the 1964 revolution were more dire as tens of thousands of women, men and children were murdered, raped, imprisoned and tortured simply for being 'the wrong' race, ethnicity or political adherence.

It has been easy in Tanzania to turn legitimate and not so legitimate political grievances into racial recriminations. Zanzibar represents a prime example where this has been done, and more so in respect to the overthrow of a legitimately elected government by so-termed 'revolutionaries' in 1964. Nyerere, his government, his party and his peers sought to explain a complex political terrain in Zanzibar in simplistic racial terms, that is, the overthrow of the minority Arab population by a majority African population aggrieved by the former's continued political domination. However, the problem lay in the electoral system in place which made it hard for a single party to have a clear majority. Consequently, before independence three successive elections saw the African majority in the isles unable to accede to political power in the face of an electoral system which was based not on the popular vote but rather on seats won, a situation similar to that seen with Al Gore and George W. Bush in the 2000 US presidential election.

Particularly significant was the categorisation of races in pre-independence Tanganyika where the key racial groups were presented as African, European and Asian. This would continue after independence as Nyerere too confined racial issues to Africans, Asians and whites, and less so to Arabs and other minority groups. Such classification is interesting in view of the large Arab population on the mainland relative to the other two minority groups and is perhaps indicative of the group's perceived political and economic insignificance compared to the situation in Zanzibar where they were a visible minority. Mwalimu's critics such as Amani Thani Fairooz (1995) and Khatib M. Rajab al-Zinjibari, however, interpret this as an aversion towards Islam as personified in the Arab. I will explore this in greater detail in the next part of this essay, but at this juncture it suffices to point out that Nyerere's inability to check or condemn the killings that followed the Zanzibar revolution is perceived as a major failure in his efforts to uphold his non-racial political agenda.

Racial politics persist in Tanzania and are largely informed by ethnicities and the question of resources and the control and ownership thereof. On the mainland, in particular, racial politics are primarily directed at the Asian population, the economic moguls. During the nationalisation campaign in the late 1960s they were the primary targets of the state takeover of private enterprises and homes; it is estimated that more than 75 per cent of the country's retail trade was controlled by Asians. Some owned factories, department stores and small shops, while others comprised the artisan class of carpenters, plumbers or tradesmen. A few become millionaires from large plantations and financial transactions.

Asian-Tanzanians have not been able to shake off the image of the scrupulous money lender or economic opportunist in the present multiparty dispensation. If anything, Asians today are accused of using their economic clout to exert political influence. The media has perpetuated this image of the un-patriotic Asian during general elections by creating an impression of a mass exodus of Asian bodies and capital. Such images are in sharp contrast to the role played by notable Asians in early political life such as Rattansy, Karimjee and Mustafa, who were revered for their dedication and sacrifice. Thus the present war on corruption is disproportionately blamed on Asians, heightening their vulnerability as a racial group.

Nyerere, religious values and vices

If corruption and greed did not taint Nyerere's political image, religious matters did. This was in spite of the fact that Nyerere, a Catholic, did not shy from wearing the Swahili skullcap to show his level of comfort with Islam. The United States Agency for International Development (USAID) avers that Nyerere adopted polices designed to minimise ethnic, religious and regional tensions and to foster an overarching sense of national unity. Accordingly, Nyerere was strict on the separation of church and state (see Ssekitooleko 2008). His socialist legacy promoted common secular values of unity, togetherness and social welfare geared at building a unified and uniform nation.

Ssekitooleko (2008) and Malambugi (2007) claim that Nyerere did not allow his religious beliefs to influence national policy, something that allowed Tanzania to experience stability, outlive all forms of sectarianism and become a secular country where religion and ethnicity would be private issues. This is a view that is not shared by all Nyerere critics. In fact, a growing amount of the literature paints a conflicting picture of Nyerere's rhetoric and practice with respect to religious beliefs, observance and practice, as will be discussed below. It is useful at this juncture to put Nyerere's association with religion into perspective, lest we fall into similar trappings as those who would not fault Nyerere and who would elevate him to super-human status.

One writer reminds us that Nyerere's sawn-off front teeth indicated his pagan, tribal background. His first encounter with major world religions was when he enrolled in school at 12 years old.

He would be baptised on 23 December 1943, at the age of 20, by Father Mathias Koenen in the Roman Catholic Church just before he went off to Makerere University. At Makerere he became one of the leaders of the Catholic students, organising retreats and pilgrimages to the shrines of the Ugandan martyrs. This interest in his faith would grow when he went to Edinburgh University.

Upon his return from Makerere, Nyerere taught at St Mary's School, owned by the Roman Catholic Church in Tabora. Similarly, upon his return from Scotland he would again teach at St Francis Secondary School, Pugu. This was the first territorial secondary school set up by the Roman Catholic hierarchy for Tanganyika. It was the elite Catholic secondary school that received the selection of all the best students when they completed middle school.

Perhaps, in view of his humble background, Nyerere felt indebted to the church. After all, it was his friends, in some cases his mentors at the church, who had raised the money for his scholarship to Makerere and later to Scotland. At a certain point in his life Nyerere considered becoming a priest but was dissuaded by Father Richard Walsh, who advised him to continue pursuing his interest in politics. The church and in particular the Fabian movement would continue to have a deep impact and role in his political life.

Even as a politician, Nyerere practiced his Christian faith openly, attending early mass whenever he could. His passion and interest in Christianity is evident in his scholarship where he is credited with translating some books of the Bible into Kizanaki, as well as into Kiswahili. Only MacDonald (1966) suggests that Nyerere was paid for translating this work, but the account of Father Arthur Wille tends to suggest that the nominal sum he received was to compensate him for his job loss at Pugu. Father Wille further reveals that Nyerere translated two catechisms, two explanations of the catechism that the white fathers had made up in Kikwaya, all the prayers for mass and all the scripture readings for mass. In 1996 he wrote poetry and spiritual songs inspired by the gospels of Matthew, Mark, Luke, John, and the acts of the Apostles in the Bible.

It is, therefore, not farfetched to assume that Nyerere's faith was central to who he is and his politics. Earlier on he is reported to have told Father Wille, 'I am not a communist – I believe in

God' when accused of belonging to the Left. Nor was he fond of members of his cabinet who espoused communism such as Abdul-Rahman Babu, Kassim Hanga and their sympathisers. Essentially, Nyerere's religious values informed his strong stance against discrimination, which he likened 'to eating the flesh of another human being', a biblical expression.

In due course, he may have compromised on socialism as a middle way between his religious beliefs and political convictions. An African brand of socialism expressed in a terminology of creed believes in the equality of men and their right to dignity and respect, and that all humans, regardless of their differences, are the purpose and justification for the existence of society, and all human activity in any given society. This philosophy demands that communities everywhere enjoy and develop themselves within the context of freedom and democracy based upon good governance and social justice, policies that are not in opposition to church doctrine.

It is significant that Nyerere's religious allegiances and actions remain hotly contested. Two trends are discernible: literature condemning his actions and practices and defences against those accusations. In my view, these trends are unhelpful in that they fail to acknowledge the struggle, personal or public, that Nyerere as a political actor went through to reconcile his beliefs with his political convictions. Moreover, they fail to provide an insight into how a public figure who is a member of a certain congregation works from that realisation to infuse a more positive engagement with national issues.

Perhaps part of the dilemma before Nyerere was his perceived support of a religious institution previously associated with maintaining the status quo, considering that the churches in Tanganyika, according to Rajab al-Zinjibari, rejected TANU, twice in 1958 at Sumbawanga and in 1965 at Mbulu. Instead, they were scheming hand-in-glove with the British colonial government, which was grooming Nyerere to be the first president of Tanganyika. In fact, just as Nyerere is seen not to distinguish the Arab from Islam, Muslim critics cannot separate his close ties to the church to the sustained promotion of a Christian agenda in his political and socio-economic policies.

But Nyerere's relationship with the church is not as black and white as some critics would suggest. In fact, Nyerere grappled with the question of a new role for the church in a new era of political dispensation. He wanted the church to serve all people, Christians and non-believers. Likewise, he wanted the church to serve the whole person, mentally, spiritually and physically, and therefore saw an expanded role for the church through activities such as running schools, hospitals and income-generating projects, and not simply proselytising.

Certainly, it could not be missed by Nyerere that at one point the Roman Catholic leadership in charge of St Francis School at Pugu, where he was teaching, asked him to choose between teaching at their school and his work in politics. It is, therefore, no wonder that in his political life he would challenge the church to remember its responsibility to society, calling for the church to recognise the need for a social revolution and to play a leading role in it (Nyerere 1974, p. 98). In this vein Nyerere did not hesitate to nationalise mission schools in an attempt to secularise the institutions in order to expand educational opportunities to non-Christian students. Education would be a key strategy to realise his vision towards a unified nation.

Imputing the religious to Nyerere

If religion was off-limits during President Nyerere's tenure, it is very much present in his life after his passing. A connection with a religious agenda is palpable in the writings available on Nyerere by both Muslim and Christian writers. Christian (especially church-based) writers want to associate Nyerere's Christian values with his particular brand of politics, whereas Muslim writers point out such influence as blinding his worldview and preventing a more rational form of political culture from emerging. Academic writers on the other hand tend to support a move towards closer scrutiny of Nyerere's policies and deeds, possibly to better appreciate the complexity he represented as a political leader.

More interesting is the tendency to apply religious imagery or to converse in religious discourse of and about Nyerere. For instance, it is telling that in one of the countless obituaries posted after his death, Nyerere should be described in the following terms: 'Julius Nyerere: political messiah or false prophet?' This image of Nyerere as saviour produced a counter-narrative that seeks to replace Nyerere with a Muslim messiah in the form of Abdul Wahid Sykes, emphasising a male-centric notion of leadership on the one hand and exposing entrenched yet silent religious misgivings on the other.

Throughout his life Nyerere was known to most Tanzanians as *Mwalimu* ('The Teacher'). Upon his retirement he was granted the title of *Baba wa Taifa* ('Father of the Nation'), a concept of fatherhood probably meant to capture his status as an elder in African society. Nevertheless, it is impossible to miss the connotation the term 'Father' has in the church. Descriptions by veteran journalists like James Mpinga, who describes the ritual of Nyerere 'breaking bread' with children in his hometown every morning, evoke in the minds of non-Christians the preoccupation of the church in making Nyerere not a national figure but a Christian figure, defeating his own dream of creating a unified nation not consumed by religious figures or preoccupations. Of course, ongoing efforts to canonise Nyerere serve to confirm suspicions that Nyerere was not a disinterested party in religious matters.

Accordingly, numerous publications reviewed zealously credit Nyerere with achievements purportedly forming part of a grand divine plan. Muslims, for their part, oppose the image of Nyerere as the single-handed liberator of Tanganyika and question the ambivalent role of missionary-educated Tanganyikans in the liberation struggle. Other allegations are less conspicuous. For example, Malambugi (2007) alleges that for the sake of religious tolerance, Nyerere helped to formulate articles guaranteeing freedom of religion in the Tanzanian constitution.

Of course, the above account differs from that given by Rajab al-Zinjibari, who observes that the constitution drafted by the British colonialists – which was unilaterally used by the Tanganyikan government as the Interim Constitution of Tanzania – did not contain freedom of religion as an independent clause, to the detriment of the Islamic state of Zanzibar. The sensitivity of religion in local politics is acknowledged by authors like Frieder Ludwig (1996 and 1999) and David Westerlund (1996), among others.

Church-affiliated writers also advance the idea that Nyerere's efforts to cultivate mutual relationships with and between

Christian and Muslim religious leaders have ensured religious tolerance in Tanzania since independence. However, authors such as Amani Thani Fairooz (1995), Khatib M. Rajab al-Zinjibari and Mohammed Said (1998) see Nyerere as a serious bulwark against the flourishing of Islam in Tanzania. First and foremost they take issue with the close association between Islam and slavery in the persona of the Arab in the country's political rhetoric and condemn the elevation of the role of the missionary and its institutions in Tanganyika's liberation.

Additionally, they accuse Mwalimu of relenting to the churches' wishes in decisions detrimental to Muslims in Tanzania. To back their claims they list various incidents where Muslim leaders and institutions were been singled out by Nyerere, seriously compromising Muslim progress in Tanzania. Chief among them is the expulsion of numerous Tanganyikan Muslims from the executive leadership of TANU. Also, the incarceration of political, religious and community Muslim figures at various times in Tanzania's political history evidenced an uncomfortable relationship between Nyerere and Muslims.

Nyerere clamped down hard on Muslim institutions, beginning by banning the All Muslim National Union of Tanzania and later the Muslim Education Union on 25 February 1965, an institution founded to train Muslims who were not allowed into the government primary schools. In 1968 he banned the East African Muslims Welfare Society (EAMWS) (Ludwig 1999). Whereas political dissent among Muslims was stifled during Nyerere's reign, the right to the free expression of the church – the Catholic Church in particular – was unhindered and constituted a formidable source of critique against government policy, such as in Christian publications like *Letter to my Superiors* (see Sivalon 1992; Mukandala et al 2006; Anderson 1977).

Such singling out can, however, be contested as it was not just Muslims who were snubbed by Nyerere. Such a fate also befell some of his close friends such as Oscar Kambona and Chief David Kidaha Makwaia, the latter a Roman Catholic. One of the most influential chiefs in East Africa, Chief Makwaia facilitated the political rise of his long-time college friend Julius Nyerere by winning him British support as well as by securing the allegiance of Sukuma chiefs to TANU. Upon attaining *uhuru*, Nyerere abolished the role of chiefs and banished Chief Makwaia to the remote Tunduru District of the southern province for undisclosed reasons (Amkpa 2007). Kambona for his part was in exile in Britain, unable to return to Tanzania until after Nyerere resigned both the presidency and party leadership.

Nevertheless, an anti-Islam agenda can still be imputed to Nyerere. He is, for instance, quoted in the book *Development and Religion in Tanzania* by J.P. van Bergen (1981) as saying that he established in TANU a department of political education at the head of which he deliberately appointed a Christian minister, Reverend Mushendwa, not because he was a strong politician but because of his Catholic faith. Also, while Nyerere was well aware of disparities between Muslims and Christians in areas of education, executive appointments and social organisation he did very little to bring about structural transformation, such that the disparities not only persisted but 40 years after independence continue to be explainable as part of the country's historical legacy.

Alhaj Aboud Jumbe, the second president of Zanzibar who, among others, fell out with Nyerere in 1984 similarly criticises Nyerere's religious policies. In his 1994 book *The Partnership: Tanganyika–Zanzibar Union: 30 Turbulent Years*, Jumbe asserts that 'Muslims were deliberately under-represented in education' and provides statistics to back up his assertion. He indicates that this 'could be a source of future conflict between Muslims and Christians' (Jumbe 1994, p. 120). The USAID-sponsored 'Conflict flashpoints in Tanzania' by M.F. Lofchie and R. Payne (1999) notes that an increasing number of Tanzanians are excluded from mainstream political and economic life, a section of society (i.e., Muslims) which perceives its exclusion on the basis of its social and religious identity. Such concerns were also captured at the advent of multiparty politics in 1995 by one M.I. Marisi in a letter to an editor entitled *Tusiwatete wanasiasa kwa misingi ya dini* ('Let religion not dictate our affiliation to political leaders'). Surely, the voicing of such concerns indicates continued vestiges of religious divisions even after over two decades of single-party dominance propounding a people-centred socialist ideology.

Redefining racial and religious tolerance

Current Tanzanian President Jakaya Mrisho Kikwete, in a speech delivered at Boston University, USA, on 25 September 2006, reiterated the dominant position with regard to Mwalimu's legacy in managing religious diversity in a democratic environment (Kikwete 2006). President Kikwete attributed to the remarkable foresight of Mwalimu Nyerere specific actions taken to engender tolerance in matters of faith and in managing potential cracks in the Tanzania nation, mainly through equitable policies, institutional innovations, political messages and legal constitutional provisions. But sustained objections, raised by diverse voices, put such allegations to question. And as feelings of exclusion intensify and disparities between Muslims and Christians continue unabated, many questions are being asked about this 'bag puzzle' (Rajab al-Zinjibari).

It is inescapable that race and religion are inextricably linked in the minds of Tanzanians, such as colonialism as being of Christian origin and slavery of Islamic origin, or Tanganyika being a missionary bastion and Zanzibar a Muslim bastion. Certainly, Tanzania's inability to overcome vestiges of racial and religious exclusion exposes the government and the ruling party's inability (or unwillingness) to address in a forthright and objective manner the racial and religious discrimination that continues to dominate Tanzania's political culture. Can such reluctance be understood as promoting tolerance? More importantly, the fixation with Muslim versus Christian in a democratic society begs the question of the status of other Tanzanians who are neither Muslim nor Christian. Do they not also have legitimate grievances premised on their right of belief or non-belief?

Nyerere's policies may have been conceived to promote national unity, but undue preoccupation with the suppression of conflict in order to compel cooperation across ethnic, religious and racial lines may have stifled genuine coexistence and the positive acknowledgement of difference in Tanzania's multiracial and multi-religious society from evolving. Inherent racial and religious tensions have become more pronounced from the early 1990s, resulting in the sowing of seeds of discord among the people and communities given that, as argued by Chachage and Chachage (2003, p.11), it defends a politics of exclusion and inclusion, privileges and denials whereby '[c]itizenship, rather than nationalism, patriotism and pan-Africanism become the real stuff'.

Perhaps then Tanzania's current political outlook stifles the possibility of a unified nation, one that accepts differences in race, religion and indeed opinion as integral to its political legacy. The challenge for future inter- and intra-racial and religious relations rests on the nation's ability to overcome racial and religious suspicion, as well as its ability to acknowledge residual institutional and individual biases impeding in the country's quest to forge a collective future.

Bibliography

Africa News Online (1999) 'Nyerere: the early years', 8 November

Amkpa, A. (2007) 'Chief David Kidaha Makwaia: Tanzanian politician, businessman and head of the Sukuma', *Guardian* (UK), 31 May

Anderson, W.B. (1977) *The Church in East Africa 1840–1974*, Central Tanganyika Press, Dar es Salaam

Anon (2007) 'Julius Kambarage Nyerere (1922–1999): statesman and pan-African leader', 1 October, http://www.nathanielturner.com/juliuskambaragenyerere.htm, accessed 4 January 2010

Boddy-Evans, A., 'A selection of quotes by Julius Kambarage Nyerere', africanhistory.about.com/od/biography/a/qts-Nyerere01.htm, accessed 4 January 2010

Chachage, C.S. and Chachage, S.L.C. (2003) 'Nyerere: nationalism and post-colonial developmentalism', paper prepared for the 30th anniversary of the Council for the Development of Social Science Research in Africa (CODESRIA), 8–11 December, Dakar, Senegal, http://www.codesria.org/Links/conferences/papers/Chachage_Seithy_L_Chachage.pdf, accessed 22 December 2009

Fairooz, A.T. (1995) *Ukweli ni Huu (kusuta uwongo)*, Dubai, United Arab Emirates

Hope, A. (2007) 'Building a convivial society: insights from Nyerere and Freire', Nyerere annual lecture on lifelong learning, University of Cape Town, 29 August, http://www.icae.org.uy/eng/nyererelecturepaperannehopeaug07.pdf, accessed 4 January 2010

Jumbe, A. (1994) *The Partnership: Tanganyika–Zanzibar Union: 30 Turbulent Years*, Amana Publishers, Dar es Salaam

Kikwete, J.M. (2006) 'Managing religious diversity in a democratic environment', speech delivered by Tanzania's president at Boston University, USA, 28 September, *Guardian*, pp. v–vi, Dar es Salaam

Laurence, T. and MacRae, C. (2007) *The Dar Mutiny of 1964*, Book Guild Ltd

Lofchie, M.F. and Payne, R. (1998) 'Conflict flashpoints in Tanzania', study for USAID under Greater Horn of Africa Initiative (GHAI), October–November

Ludwig, F. (1996) 'After Ujamaa: is religious revivalism a threat to Tanzania's stability', in Westerlund, D. (ed) *Questioning the Secular State: the Worldwide Resurgence of Religion in Politics*, Hurst and Company (Publishers) Ltd., pp. 216–35

Ludwig, F. (1999) *Church and State in Tanzania: Aspects of a Changing Relationship, 1961–1994*, Brill Academic Publishers

MacDonald, A. (1966) *Tanzania: Young Nation in a Hurry*, Hawthorne Books Inc, New York

Majira (1995) 'Tusiwatete wanasiasa kwa misingi ya dini', 27 April, Dar es Salaam

Malambugi, A.I. (2007) 'Julius Kambarage Nyerere, 1922 to 1999, Roman Catholic Church, Tanzania', *Dictionary of African Christian Biography*, http://www.dacb.org/stories/tanzania/nyerere.html, accessed 22 December 2009

Mukandala, R., Yahya-Othman, S., Mushi, S. and Ndumbaro, L. (eds) (2006) *Justice, Rights and Worship: Religion and Politics in Tanzania*, Research and Education for Democracy in Tanzania (REDET), Dar es Salaam

Mwakikagile, G. (2004) *Nyerere and Africa: End of an Era*, Protea Publishing

Nyerere, J.K. (1967) *Freedom and Development*, Oxford University Press, Oxford

Nyerere, J.K. (1974) *Man and Development*, Oxford University Press, Oxford

Rajab al-Zinjibari, K.M. 'Nyerere against Islam in Zanzibar and Tanganyika', http://victorian.fortunecity.com/portfolio/543/nyerere_and_islam.htm, accessed 22 December 2009

Said, M. (1998) *The Life and Times of Abdul Wahid Sykes (1924-1968): the Untold Story of the Muslim Struggle against British Colonialism in Tanganyika*, Minerva Press

Sivalon, J. (1992) *Kanisa Katoliki na Siasa ya Tanzania Bara 1953–1985*, Benedictine Publications

Ssekitooleko, D. (2008) 'Tanzania: Julius Nyerere's secular legacy', *International Humanist and Ethical Union*, http://www.iheu.org/node/3240, accessed 22 December 2009

Time (1967) 'Africa: black resentment for the Asians', 24 February, http://www.time.com/time/magazine/article/0,9171,899418-1,00.html, accessed 22 December 2009

Van Bergen, J.P. (1981) *Development and Religion in Tanzania: Sociological Soundings on Christian Participation in Rural Transformation*, Christian Literature Society, Leiden, IIMO/Madras

Westerlund, D. (ed) (1996) *Questioning the Secular State: The Worldwide Resurgence of Religion in Politics*, London, C. Hurst & Co

Wille, A. 'Maryknoll and politics in Tanzania', http://www.maryknollafrica.org/History10.htm, accessed 22 December 2009

Mwalimu Nyerere and the challenge of human rights

Helen Kijo-Bisimba and Chris Maina Peter

Introduction: the complexity of the subject

It is not easy to write about Mwalimu Nyerere and human rights without sounding and looking rather confused and ridiculous. This is because Mwalimu's position is highly complex. Here one is confronted by two quite different personalities. There is Mwalimu the individual, a God-fearing and religious family person who respects and champions the rights of all people. Then there is the other Mwalimu – the president of the united republic – signing a few death warrants, detaining people in custody without trial by applying the 1962 Preventive Detention Act[1], and deporting citizens of Tanzania from one part of the country to another by invoking an old colonial law, the Deportation Ordinance of 1938.[2]

It is also true that some of the negative aspects of Mwalimu's time in office are underplayed because by all standards he was the best president that Tanzania has ever had, and maybe will ever have. He set such high standards that all his successors look like dwarfs before the performance of the master.

Mwalimu was a patriot. He considered himself first as an African and then second as Tanzanian. He valued the general and not the particular. For him, the general was the community and the particular the individual. In his opinion, the community was far more important than the individual. The individual could be sacrificed, but not the community. It is this philosophical position which was clearly reflected in his position on human rights. This was both at an individual level as Mwalimu Julius Nyerere or as head of state. What is important was the fact that he never wavered. He said what he believed in and practised the same.

Mwalimu's background and individual rights

As an individual, Mwalimu was deeply religious. This made him a moderate person. He had enormous powers in a newly independent state. The majority of the people were ignorant but he never at any point in time attempted to take advantage of them and of the high office he occupied. He worried about them and their future throughout his tenure as head of state.

One of the strongest beliefs guiding him in his work and in his interaction with other people was the equality of all human beings. This belief runs through all his writings, speeches and arguments. It was the cardinal rule in the constitution of the Tanganyika African National Union (TANU), the nationalist party he and others established in 1954 and which led the country to independence in 1961. The same sentiments about the equality of all human beings are to be found in the Arusha Declaration of 1967[3] and in the policies that followed on agriculture and education.[4] It is also this deep belief in the equality of human beings that guided Mwalimu in his approach to human rights.

Mwalimu articulated this position well:

> The people and the Government of the United Republic are aiming to build a just society of free and equal citizens, who live in healthy conditions, who control their own destiny, and who cooperate together and with other people in a spirit of human brotherhood for mutual benefit. This is the goal.[5]

The equality of all human beings made Mwalimu question colonialism, apartheid and other policies which promoted class differentiation in human beings. Thus Mwalimu became the backbone of the liberation struggle in southern Africa and the front line states. He invited and hosted freedom fighters in the country without any question. All these actions were guided by his belief in the equality of all human beings.

The individual versus the community

Much as Mwalimu loved human beings and wanted them to be treated equally and without any discrimination, he did not do that blindly. He was guided by the need to give priority to the community over the individual. Therefore, unlike most of the western thinkers and philosophers in the human rights field who gave priority to individual rights, Mwalimu relegated them to a lower level. For him, the rights of the majority – the community and their rights – were his priority, and not the individual.

It is therefore not surprising that when the heads of state and government of the Organisation of African Unity (OAU) decided to establish a human rights regime, Mwalimu's influence could not be missed. In the human rights document adopted in Nairobi in 1981 – the African Charter on Human and Peoples' Rights – community rights, in the form of peoples' rights, were adopted for the first time in an international treaty. The rights falling under this category included the right to peace, the right to self-determination and the right to a clean and satisfactory environment.[6]

Violations of rights under Mwalimu's rule

Notwithstanding the fact that Mwalimu was highly religious, loved the people and so on, fingers continue to be pointed towards the many incidents of violations of human rights in Tanzania during his reign as head of state. It was under Mwalimu that the nationalists negotiating for the independence of Tanganyika in London and Dar es Salaam rejected the inclusion of a bill of rights in the independence constitution of 1961. The same position was repeated during the Republican Constitution of 1962, the Interim Constitution of 1965 and the Permanent Constitution of the United Republic of Tanzania of 1977. The Bill of Rights was eventually incorporated in the constitution in 1984 due to pressure from the people.[7] That was a year before he voluntary left office.

Apart from rejecting a bill of rights which could have guaranteed most of the fundamental rights and freedoms of the individual, it has also been pointed out that Mwalimu supported the extension and use of some of the oppressive colonial laws and allowed the enactment of new laws which also curtailed freedoms and the rights of individuals.

Among the colonial legislation allowed to continue in use was the Penal Code of 1945, the Collective Punishment Ordinance of 1921, the Townships (Removal of Undesirable Persons) Ordinance of 1944 and the Deportation Ordinance of 1938, which allowed the head of state to deport citizens from one part of the country to another. This law was to be declared unconstitutional by the High Court of Tanzania in the case of *Chumchua s/o Marwa v. Officer i/c Musoma Prison and Another* in 1988.[8] Controversial legislation enacted by the government with Mwalimu at the helm includes the Preventive Detention Act of 1962, which allowed detention without due process and was discussed at length in the 1979 case of *Ahmed Janmohamed Dhirani v. Republic,*[9] along with the Regions and Regional Commissioners Act of 1962 and the Areas and Area Commissioners Act of the same year, which allowed these two important representatives of the government in the regions to curtail the freedoms of the individual for specific periods, again without due process.[10]

It has also been pointed out that apart from legislation, Mwalimu and his ruling party declared one-party rule, thus curtailing the rights of the people to organise and to form and join political parties of their own choice. It is not only political parties which were curtailed but also civil society organisations, which were also organised around the party along with mass organisations under the party. These were for workers, women, youth, parents and cooperatives. It is argued that if Mwalimu was a democrat, then why did he block all routes to people's freedoms?

Another issue for which Mwalimu is blamed and which is indicated as a clear violation of the rights of the people was the villagisation programme of 1970s. This programme involved moving thousands of citizens around the country into over 10,000 villages established around the country.[11] This movement of people was not voluntary. According to the Honourable Mr Justice Mnzavas:

> [O]peration vijiji was implemented with high-handedness. Objections were not allowed. The role of those affected by operation vijiji 1974 was not to reason why. Theirs was but to comply, the irrationality of the operation notwithstanding.[12]

The whole operation, though said to have been done in good faith, strongly undermined the image of the country and that of its leader Mwalimu Nyerere and his record of promoting and protecting human rights. Years later, some would sue the government for what happened to their property in the process of implementing this political policy.[13]

Evaluating Mwalimu and human rights

It is important to concede that all the complaints made against Mwalimu are valid. That is to say, these events did take place and they are not fabrications. However, they have explanations. They were not the actions of a dictator wanting to oppress his people in order to stay in power by all means, as is the case in most states around the African continent.

It is almost impossible to indicate any personal gain or interest in anything which Mwalimu did. It is the interests of the wider community which guided Mwalimu in his decisions and actions. At times, when the wider interests of the community and those of the individual clashed, Mwalimu made his choice. There certainly were complaints.

At times, Mwalimu agonised to explain. For instance, trying to justify the existence of detention without trial through the Preventive Detention Act of 1962, he said:

> Take the question of detention without trial. This is a desperately serious matter. It means that you are imprisoning a man when he has not broken any written law, or when you cannot be sure of proving beyond reasonable doubt that he has done so. You are restricting his liberty, making him suffer materially and spiritually, for what you believe he intends to do, or is trying to do, or for what you believe he has done. Few things are more dangerous to the freedom of a society than that. For freedom is indivisible, and with such opportunity open to the Government of the day, the freedom of every citizen is reduced. To suspend the Rule of Law under any circumstances is to leave open the possibility of the grossest injustices being perpetrated.[14]

Mwalimu then goes on to justify the use of this harsh law as a means of preventing a handful of individuals from putting the nation in jeopardy and reducing to ash the efforts of millions. He further adds that 'it becomes a question of emphasis and priorities'. This statement by Mwalimu summarises his position on the individual versus the wider community.

Mwalimu and women's rights

Mwalimu thought and exercised women's rights long before many women's rights activists began to campaign on those rights.

Sharp as he was intellectually, Mwalimu noted quite early the unjustifiable discrimination of women as women in various societies – a fact which no sane person can deny. He was able to note the unequal position occupied by men and women in the production process. While women worked on land, most traditions and cultures – particularly in Africa – did not allow them to own land and other instruments of production. Men have almost total control of both the means of production and the production process itself. While it may be true that they acquired this through hard labour and industry within the division of labour in society, their current performance, particularly in the rural areas, hardly justifies the privileged position which they still occupy. This situation is graphically noted by Mwalimu, who said:

> [T]he truth is that in the villages women work very hard. At times they work for twelve or fourteen hours. They even work on Sundays and public holidays. Women who live in villages work harder than everybody else in Tanzania. *But men who live in villages … are on leave for half of their lives.*[15]

This form of social arrangement does not in any way justify the power which men in the rural areas have over the rest of the people and women in particular.

In his writings Mwalimu emphasised equality between men and women, underlining the need for women to enjoy rights as fellow citizens and stressing that for the development of the country women had to be given a chance to exercise their rights. On the issue of education for all, Mwalimu made a strong insistence on giving girls a chance to be educated. It is therefore understandable that he wasted no time in supporting the Lindi Resolution of the Umoja wa Wanawake wa Tanzania (UWT), which argued that girls should be allowed to join the institutions of higher learning immediately after national service without having to wait for two years like boys. This resolution was endorsed by the then single ruling party, the Tanganyika African National Union (TANU), under the chairmanship of Mwalimu. Thus in 1977 girls flooded the institutions of higher learning, a development which was adopted as a general rule and which Mwalimu insisted was necessary in order to redress a historical marginalisation.[16]

At the same time, Mwalimu's views and writings on the equality of all human beings in general and gender equality in particular influenced various sections of society. Among the areas influenced by Mwalimu was the judiciary, which is by tradition known to be highly conservative. For instance, in the case of *Bernado Ephraim v. Holaria Pastory and Gervazi Kaizilege,* which was addressing the Haya customary law which denied women the right to inherit land,[17] Honourable Mr Justice James Mwalusanya relied heavily on Mwalimu's thinking on equality. The judge quoted with approval the booklet 'Socialism and rural development' where Mwalimu had rejected discrimination of women, saying:

> ... although every individual was joined to his fellow by human respect, there was in most parts of Tanzania, an acceptance of one human inequality. Although we try to hide the fact and despite the exaggeration which our critics have frequently indulged in, it is true that the women in traditional society were regarded as having a place in the community which was not only different, but was also to some extent inferior. This is certainly inconsistent with our socialist conception of the equality of all human beings and the right of all to live in such security and freedom as is consistent with equal security and freedom from all other. If we want our country to make full and quick progress now, it is essential that our women live in terms of full equality with their fellow citizens who are men.[18]

The judge thus declared Haya customary law, which discriminated against women, unconstitutional. And there were many other cases where Mwalimu and his thinking were taken as persuasive authority by different judges in the courts of law to reach just decisions.[19]

Mwalimu, retirement and human rights

Interestingly, in retirement Mwalimu became almost like an activist. He criticised the government of the day for actions he himself seemed to do with ease during his time as president. It would seem that retirement gave the former president time to reflect on many issues he had taken for granted while in office. Also, Mwalimu, unlike many of his contemporaries, studied carefully the signs and the mood of the times.

It is therefore not surprising that Mwalimu was the force behind the re-introduction of the multiparty political system in Tanzania in 1992, which came following the recommendations of the Nyalali Commission. Supporting the decision of the High Court of Tanzania in the case of Reverend Christopher Mtikila on the role of independent candidates in elections in Tanzania, Mwalimu also spiritedly argued for the country to allow people who were not necessarily supported by political parties to stand for elections. Unfortunately, to date, the ruling party has blocked this avenue for accessing public office.

Conclusion

There is no doubt that Mwalimu Nyerere and human rights will remain a controversial topic. For those wanting to study this topic further, two issues are important. First, appreciating Mwalimu's strong and unwavering position on the equality of all human beings as his guiding principle, and second, the clear distinction between the individual and the community.

Mwalimu loved the community – the general as opposed to the individual. Whatever Mwalimu did that could be interpreted as violating human rights can always be explained in the wider benefits to the community. Also gratifying is the fact that later in life Mwalimu was honest in conceding and acknowledging mistakes and making good on them. Few human beings are capable of doing that.

Notes

1. According to Cranford Pratt, the Preventive Detention Act was an authoritarian instrument available to the government for the disciplining and the restraining of its critics. See C. Pratt (1976) *The Critical Phase in Tanzania*

1945–1968: Nyerere and the Emergence of a Socialist Strategy, Cambridge, Cambridge University Press, p. 187.

2. On these two and other pieces of legislation in Tanzania permitting detention without trial and due process see C.M. Peter (1993) 'Preventive detention and security law in Tanzania', in A. Harding and J. Hatchard (eds) *Preventive Detention and Security Law: A Comparative Survey*, Dordrecht, The Netherlands, Martinus Nijhoff Publishers, p. 247.

3. Following the adoption of the Arusha Declaration in 1967, the government nationalised all the major means of production and exchange, thus affecting the right to private property. Part of this important political pronouncement is reproduced in J.K. Nyerere (1970) 'The Arusha Declaration and TANU's policy of socialism and self-reliance', in I.L. Markovitz (1970) *African Politics and Society: Basic Issues and Problems of Government and Development*, New York and London, The Free Press and Collier-Macmillan Limited, p. 266; and S.E. Chambua (1994) 'The development debates and the crisis of development theories: the case of Tanzania with special emphasis on peasants, state and capital', in U. Himmelstrand, K. Kinyanjui and E. Mburugu (eds), *African Perspectives on Development: Controversies, Dilemmas and Openings*, Nairobi, Dar es Salaam, Harare, Kampala, New York and London, East African Educational Publishers, Mkuki na Nyota, Boabab, Fountain Publishers, St Martin's Press and James Currey, p. 37 and p. 45.

4. On these policies, which went hand in hand with the Arusha Declaration, see J.K. Nyerere (1968) *Freedom and Socialism: a Selection from Writings and Speeches 1965–1967*, Dar es Salaam, Oxford University Press, pp. 337–66; and P.K. Kimiti (not dated) 'Siasa ya TANU katika kilimo', Dar es Salaam, National Printing Company, cited in D.E. McHenry, Jr. (1979) *Tanzania's Ujamaa Villages: the Implementation of a Rural Development Strategy*, Berkeley, Institute of International Studies, University of California, p. 103.

5. J.K. Nyerere (1966) *Freedom and Unity*, Dar es Salaam, Oxford University Press, p. 311.

6. On the African Charter on Human and Peoples' Rights and its contribution to the better appreciation of human rights in general see Issa G. Shivji (1989) *The Concept of Human Rights in Africa*, Dakar, CODESRIA; M. Hamalengwa et al (eds) (1988) *The International Law of Human Rights in Africa: Basic Documents and Annotated Bibliography*, Dordrecht, Boston and London, Martinus Nijhoff Publishers; O.C. Eze (1984) *Human Rights in Africa: Some Selected Problems*, Lagos, Nigerian Institute of International Affairs and Macmillan Nigeria Publishers Ltd; N.S. Rembe (1991) 'The system of protection of human rights under the African Charter on Human and Peoples' Rights: problems and prospects', *Human and Peoples' Rights Monograph Series*, no. 6, Roma, Lesotho, Institute of Southern African Studies, National University of Lesotho; and C.M. Peter (1990) *Human Rights in Africa: A Comparative Study of the African Human and Peoples' Rights Charter and the New Tanzanian Bill of Rights*, New York, Westport, Connecticut, and London, UK, Greenwood Press.

7. Even then, the Bill of Rights was suspended for three years, allegedly to give the government time to put its house in order before operationalising

the bill. This suspension of the justifiability of the Bill of Rights was done through the Constitution (Consequential, Transitional and Temporary Provisions) Act of 1984 (Act No. 16), which in Section 5 (2) provided, inter alia, that: 'Notwithstanding the amendment of the Constitution and, in particular, the justiciability of the provisions relating to basic rights, freedoms and duties, no existing law or any other provision in any existing law may, until after three years from the date of the commencement of the Act, be construed by any court in the United Republic as being unconstitutional or otherwise inconsistent with any provision of the Constitution.' See D.Z. Lubuva (1988) 'Reflections on Tanzanian Bill of Rights,' *Commonwealth Law Bulletin*, vol. 14, no. 2, p. 853.

8. J. Mwalusanya (1988) Miscellaneous criminal case, High Court of Tanzania at Mwanza, no. 2 (unreported).

9. J. Maganga (1976) Miscellaneous criminal case, High Court of Tanzania at Mwanza, no. 28, reported in 1979 LRT no. 1. These cases and others are analysed in C.M. Peter (1997) *Human Rights in Tanzania: Selected Cases and Materials*, Cologne, Germany, Rüdiger Köppe Verlag; and H. Kijo-Bisimba and C.M. Peter (eds) (2005) *Justice and Rule of Law in Tanzania: Selected Judgements and Writings of Justice James L. Mwalusanya and Commentaries*, Dar es Salaam, Legal and Human Rights Centre.

10. These oppressive laws were condemned by the Nyalali Commission on Single or Multiparty System in its report of 1991 which characterised the laws as the '40-plus laws' to be addressed. According to the commission, some should be amended while others should be repealed altogether. See Government of the United Republic of Tanzania (1992) *The Report and Recommendations of the Presidential Commission on Single Party or Multiparty System in Tanzania, 1991 on the Democratic System in Tanzania*, vol. 3, Dar es Salaam, Dar es Salaam University Press.

11. On how this programme was carried out see, inter alia, J.V. Mwapachu (1979) 'Operation planned villages in rural Tanzania: a revolutionary strategy for development' in A. Coulson (ed), *African Socialism in Practice: the Tanzanian Experience*, Nottingham, Spokesman, p. 114.

12. In the case of *Mohamed Hassan Hole v. Keya Jumanne Ramadhan* (1992) Court of Appeal of Tanzania at Dodoma, civil appeal no. 19 (unreported).

13. See for instance the case of *Attorney-General v. Lohay Akonaay and Another* (1994) Court of Appeal of Tanzania at Arusha, civil appeal no. 31, Nyalali, C.J., reported in [1995] 2 LRC 399, where the Court of Appeal of Tanzania justified and defended the villagisation programme.

14. J.K. Nyerere (1966) *Freedom and Unity*, Dar es Salaam, Oxford University Press, p. 312.

15. See J.K. Nyerere (1968) *Freedom and Socialism: a Selection from Writings and Speeches 1965–1967*, Dar es Salaam, Oxford University Press, p. 245. On the interpretation of this situation see C.M. Peter (2005) 'Liberating the slave of the slave: contribution of the new Protocol on the Rights of Women in Africa to the struggle for gender equality', in H. Scholler and S. Tellenbach (eds) *Faktoren der Enststehung und Uberwindung unfreier Arbeit in Europa und in den*

afrikanischen Kolonien, Munster, Germany, Lit Verlag, p. 57.

16. On this progressive approach to equality and other rights which the single ruling party granted women, such as fully paid maternity leave for working women, see N. Tenga and C.M. Peter (1996) 'The right to organize as mother of all rights: the experience of women organization in Tanzania', vol. 34, no. 1, *Journal of Modern African Studies*, March, p. 143; and C.M. Peter (2006) 'The state of independent civil society organisations: the case of Tanzania Women Council (BAWATA)', in A.S. Kiondo and J.E. Nyang'oro (eds) *Civil Society and Democratic Development in Tanzania*, Harare, MWENGO and Prestige Books, p.105.

17. High Court of Tanzania at Mwanza (PC), civil appeal no. 70 of 1989, reported in [1990] LRC (Const) 757.

18. This pamphlet is reproduced in J.K. Nyerere (1968) *Freedom and Socialism: a Selection from Writings and Speeches 1965-1967*, Dar es Salaam, Oxford University Press, p. 337.

19. See for instance the decisions in *Re An Application by Paul Massawe*, High Court of Tanzania at Arusha, miscellaneous civil application no. 21 of 1977 (unreported); *Ally Lilakwa v. Regional Prisons Officer Arusha and Another*, High Court of Tanzania at Arusha, miscellaneous criminal case no. 29 of 1979 (unreported); *Ntiyahela Boneka v. Kijiji cha Ujamaa Mutala*, High Court of Tanzania at Tabora, (PC) civil appeal no. 21 of 1987 (unreported); *Lalata Msangawale v. Henry Mwamlima*, High Court of Tanzania at Dodoma, civil appeal no. 99 of 1975, reported in 1979 LRT no. 3; *Laiton Kigala v. Musa Bariti*, High Court of Tanzania at Dodoma, High Court (PC) civil revision no. 148 of 1975; *Ngwegwe s/o Sangija and 3 Others v. Republic*, High Court of Tanzania at Mwanza, criminal appeal no. 72 of 1987 (unreported); and *Charles Charari Maitari v. Matiko Chacha Cheti and 4 Others*, High Court of Tanzania at Mwanza, (HC) civil case no. 15 of 1987 (unreported).

Mwalimu Nyerere: the artist

Vicensia Shule

There are many matters in Africa and beyond for which Mwalimu Julius Nyerere can be acknowledged for his contribution and participation. These range from social and political issues to international affairs. The aim of this chapter is not only to demonstrate Nyerere's intellectualism and his artistic skills, but also to show how he used the arts to express his philosophy and ideas. Employing his artistic creativity, he managed to identify the potential of the arts in building an independent nation soon after independence. This chapter discusses Nyerere as an artist and his initiatives to protect art. It also analyses how the shift of ideology from socialism to neoliberalism has affected the arts.

Historically, both the German and the British colonial governments were keen to destroy theatre and other cultural activities because for them they were 'demonic' and 'barbaric'. Germans, for example, neither established a theatre institution nor impressed their aesthetics upon the local population. 'Because of ignorance and because for the most part it suited them, they denigrated local performances as "uncivilised" activities' (Lihamba 2004, p. 236). Mollel (1985) and Lihamba (1985a) explain how the British occupation resulted in the introduction of colonial theatre in Tanganyika in the 1920s. Lihamba (2004, pp. 236–7) regards British colonialism as the beginning of 'a period of aggressive introduction of western theatre' which was 'facilitated through two major channels; schools and expatriate drama clubs'. Western theatre performed in racially segregated schools, used proscenium arch stages, and expensive costumes (Mollel 1985, p. 23).

The period between 1945 and 1952 was marked by the aggressive return of colonial theatre after a lull in the years from 1922 to 1940s, when Britain was economically 'strangled' as Chachage

(1986) elaborates. There was the re-introduction of the performance of western dramas such as those by William Shakespeare, Bernard Shaw, Gilbert and Sullivan (Lihamba 2004, p. 237). Although such western performances could not trace any roots in Africa, they were considered to be a 'universal' model of theatre, as Mollel (1985) argues. The Little Theatres were established by the British in Dar es Salaam and Arusha in 1947 and 1953 respectively. They were used as a model to show 'elite' Africans or 'black Europeans' (as Nyerere referred to them) the quality and value of western theatre (Mlama 1991, p. 100).

Missionaries and the church had a similar perception of African performing arts. Apart from their moral plays, traditional African theatre was seen as demonic and repugnant. There have been two schools of thought on why colonialists and missionaries were keen to suppress traditional African theatre in favour of western theatre. There were those scholars such as Plastow who believed that missionaries did not fully understand African performing arts and theatre. Theatre, along with other performing arts, was associated with witchcraft and was thus classified as demonic. She argues:

> Traditional performance was often related to indigenous religion, to sexuality and to alcohol – all things which the Church strove to deny the African people. Moreover, traditional African culture must have been extremely frightening to many imperialists. They generally understood neither its language nor its form, and had been so indoctrinated in the 'savage' nature of 'primitive' Africa that a firelight *ngoma* may well have been transmuted in their eyes into a pagan ritual of frightening barbarity.
>
> (Plastow 1996, p. 45)

Scholars like Bakari and Materego (2008), Kerr (1995), Mlama (1985) and Nsekela (1984) offered an alternative view. They argued that the banning was not 'an accident'. Colonialists knew that theatre was a simulacrum of culture, and the Christians suppressed African performing arts when 'they realised culture held the symbolic key to the religious and moral bases of indigenous societies' (Kerr 1995, p. 18). Nsekela (1984, p. 58) explained in detail how the colonial education provided by the missionaries was used to encourage people to accept 'human inequality and domination of the weak by the strong' as one of the fundamental elements of being civilised. Even the process of introducing missionaries to an area before establishing a colonial administration was for a specific purpose. Mlama (1985, p. 9) argued that 'in capitalist systems, the mind of the exploited was turned to accept exploitation', and religious 'songs for example, especially those of Christianity, have been extensively used by capitalists to make people accept worldly material poverty in the hope of receiving heavenly spiritual salvation'.

Before the end of World War II, cultural activities including traditional dances – *ngoma* – were seen as obscene, barbaric and one of the activities which propagated tribalism (Plastow 1996). Later in 1948, the British colonial government changed its cultural policy to allow and encourage cultural activities including *ngoma* (Rubin and Diakante 2001, p. 302). The British provided a list of 20 *ngoma* which were acceptable (Lange 1995, p. 46). This could be seen as a difference between the Germans and the British, but in actual fact the point in time when the British government decided to allow certain *ngoma* was a time when nationalism and liberation movements had begun and the colonial administration was in no position to say otherwise (Askew 2002, p. 168). This freedom was to satirically 'distract them from the mounting opposition to colonial domination in the empire' (Mlama 1991, p. 58).

Despite this attack, it was clear that the colonialists could not manage to wipe out African traditional performing arts (Lihamba 2004, p. 236). As the colonial government banned various traditional performances due to their 'barbaric' nature, certain theatre groups resisted this 'cultural invasion' and fought for their cultural freedom. *Beni ngoma* was one example of how they did this. This type of dance was developed primarily by taking various elements from existing social, political and colonial organisations. The dancers wore imitations of colonial military costumes. The music (brass band) and even the dancing itself (parade) imitated military drill practices. *Beni ngoma* performances were done under various associations. These associations were always in opposition to each other or in a 'joke partnership'. The best-known ones were Marini against Arinoti and Kingi against Scotchi (Askew 2002; Chachage 2002; Ranger 1975; Lange 2002; Edmondson 2007).

Surprisingly, the colonialists were attracted to *beni ngoma* because they saw it as evidence that Africans understood the kind of performances that the colonialists wanted them to put on. 'The imitation of European dress and drills, especially by the African civil servants, teachers and soldiers, was seen as a civilising process for the local people' (Lihamba 2004, p. 238). Thus, the notion that *ngoma* and other traditional performances were 'barbaric' was fully understood by the *beni* artists. However, *beni*, as any other theatrical form, was a result of the oppressive administrative structure imposed by the rulers, with the ruled struggling to find their own space within the administrative systems that had been created. As Ngugi (1997, p. 127) clearly shows, the consequences of any submissive domination is the birth of a culture of resistance.

Later, the colonial government decided to regulate *beni* because they thought it stimulated political consciousness as it contained elements that were abusive and which questioned the legitimacy of the colonial administration (Chachage 1986). For the colonialists, *beni* became a communist society (Lihamba 2004, p. 238). As a result, the colonial government started to charge a tax for each performance so as to discourage people from dancing. As you would expect, some members of the *beni* associations were part of the nationalist movement which gave birth to the Tanganyika African National Union (TANU), the party which fought for independence (Lihamba 1985a, pp. 29–30).

To mark the attainment of 'pseudo' independence on the eve of 9 December 1961, the Mwenge wa Uhuru (freedom/uhuru torch) was placed on the top of Mount Kilimanjaro by Alexander Nyirenda as a symbol of freedom. I would argue that the ritual of placing the torch and the annual uhuru torch race (Mbio za Mwenge wa Uhuru) represent Nyerere's appreciation of the performing arts and its role in shaping people's consciousness towards a common goal.

The establishment of the Ministry of Culture and Youth can be traced to the president's 1962 inaugural address. In this speech, Nyerere outlined the roles of the ministry, which included facilitating the process of enabling Tanzanians to regain their cultural pride (Nyerere 1966, p. 187). In the same speech to parliament, Nyerere indicated his concern about how colonialism had dehumanised African arts. His speech became the blueprint for Tanzania's cultural policy and led to various art reforms. These included the 'institutionalisation' of national art groups (NAGs). The aim of institutionalising NAGs was to fulfil Nyerere's quest for the renaissance of Africanness in the arts and culture (Bakari and Materego 2008).

The institutionalised groups included the National Ngoma Troupe (1963), the National Acrobatic Group (1969) and the National Drama Group (1972). These groups were designed to act as a model of performing arts in Tanzania. For example, the National Ngoma Troupe had 30 artists recruited from the various regions in Tanzania, both musicians and dancers (Lange 2002, p. 55). It should be noted that the process of building a national culture through theatre groups dates back to the birth of TANU in 1954 when a theatre group based on Nyamwezi dance known as Hiari ya Moyo under Suleiman Mwinamila participated effectively in creating a national theatre (Semzaba 1983). The decolonisation movement started with the beginning of TANU's formation, and Hiari ya Moyo was forced to include the concepts of nationalism and liberation in its work, in other words to fight against colonialism and (cultural) imperialism. *Amka Msilale* (Wake up, don't sleep) was their first recorded performance in 1954.

Amka Msilale	Wake up don't sleep
Msiwe wajinga mu Tanganyika	Don't be stupid, you are in Tanganyika [territory]
Tanganyika ni mali yetu	Tanganyika is our property
Tukidai tutapewa	If we demand it, we'll be given
	(Semzaba 1983, p. 22)

The multiplication of NAGs trickled down to the village level. The process did not end with their establishment; their existence was facilitated because they were seen as the foundation of national artistic pride. These groups performed in political rallies, state banquets and meetings at all levels. Members of the NAGs were state employees. Since the state subsidised most of the costs and paid for their monthly salaries, the groups were not allowed to charge or receive extra payment for their performances. The focus was on the promotion of national unity and on echoing the state's Ujamaa policies. One of the positive outcomes of such initiatives was to make active involvement in theatre possible at various levels of society (Mlama 1985, p.103).

The 'ritual' surrounding the union between Tanganyika and Zanzibar on 26 April 1964 can be seen as another artistic performance. In addition to the usual practice of signing the treaty and exchanging the Articles of Union, Nyerere mixed the soil of the two countries. Nyerere wore a shirt made of leopard skin. He used two gourds filled with soil from Tanganyika and Zanzibar. Then the mixing was done by pouring the soil in the pot. The two men who held the pot were were both kneeling and dressed in *kitenge* (cotton fabric) tailored uniforms. The costumes, props and the mixing of the soil symbolised how Nyerere valued and treasured arts and his belief in the content of traditional theatre.

Mwalimu, as Nyerere was commonly known, also produced a variety of theatre works. As part of his mission to decolonise theatre, Mwalimu translated some famous Shakespeare plays into Kiswahili. According to Rubin and Diakante (2001, p. 301) these were *Julius Caesar* as *Julius Kaizari* (1968), *Macbeth* as *Makbeth* (1968) and *The Merchant of Venice* as *Mabepari wa Venisi* (1969).

One explanation for why Nyerere translated those works could be that by unfolding what was within the famous Shakespeare's English-based theatre, he could add value to people's theatre and help them 'regain their pride'. He believed that Kiswahili readers could better understand the content and context of the Shakespeare's plays and have an opportunity to compare African/Tanzanian and foreign/western theatre in the process of regaining their pride. Secondly, for Mwalimu, it was important to promote Kiswahili as the language of theatre and nation building (Rubin and Diakante 2001, p. 302). Mazrui and Mazrui (1995, p.82) also elaborated on how Nyerere developed Kiswahili as a language for 'cultural self-reliance' and 'self development'. 'The country's first president Julius Nyerere, himself set an impressive example of competence and versatility in that language, ranging from dazzling oratory to the tough self-imposed assignments of translating Shakespeare's *Julius Caesar* and *Merchant of Venice*.' Thirdly, perhaps it was a way of proving to the world that what the majority were glorifying as 'holy' literature, a simple person – a proletarian, as he preferred to call himself – could read, understand and even translate. In fact in his 1962 speech to parliament, Nyerere lamented how European education dwelled more on teaching people how to dance the foxtrot, waltz and rock 'n' roll. He asserted that this made educated people unable to dance traditional dances such as *gombe sugu*, the *mangala*, *kiduo* or *lele mama*, and that some had not even heard of them (Nyerere 1966, p. 187).

One has to read between the lines to get a sense of Mwalimu's inner motive for translating the works. For example *The Merchant of Venice* could literally be translated as *Mfanyabiashara* (or *Wafanyabiashara* in the plural) *wa Venice*. But Nyerere chooses the word *mabepari* (*bepari* in the singular), which means capitalist(s). Mwangi (2009, pp. 170–1) regards this as a 'socialist twist' where Nyerere emphasised 'competitive and capitalistic tendencies' which were not in the original Shakespeare play. Perhaps after reading the book, Nyerere realised that the merchant's behaviour could not be differentiated from those of the capitalists. In addition, it might be that he wanted to concisely deliver the point home since, being a self-proclaimed African socialist (*mjamaa*), he was anti-capitalist. As noted, he purposely used the plural form of the title as opposed to its singular 'merchant'. It has also been observed that the years when he translated the works, between 1967 and 1969, reflect the promotion of the then dominant Ujamaa ideology, which he wanted to trickle down to people. All these translations and initiatives indicated, arguably, his stance against imperialism and its various manifestations. He saw imperialism as the cause of misconceived African history and arts. Nyerere's mission to translate philosophical pieces so as to deliver their message to the people continued up to late 1990: 'Mwalimu Nyerere's last intellectual work was the translation into Kiswahili of Plato's *The Republic*. As he was lying in bed at London's St Thomas Hospital, he went through the manuscript, made the necessary corrections and completed them before he died. Unfortunately the work has not yet been published' (Othman 2007, p. 79-80).

Mwalimu was also able to link his Ujamaa philosophy with the fine arts. The famous Makonde sculpture known as *Dimoongo* by Robert Yakobo Sangwani was renamed *Ujamaa* in the 1960s after the Arusha Declaration of 1967. *Dimoongo* demonstrated a Makonde strength or power. Looking at the way the sculptor had been able to construct one person at the bottom supporting others and how those who have been supported, support themselves as a group, translated itself to Mwalimu's idea of Ujamaa (Erick 2009). It is said that it was Mwalimu who renamed it *Ujamaa* after seeing its structure.

Besides his thought-provoking speeches, Nyerere also employed poetic creativity to address some contentious national issues. For instance, in 1993 he wrote a poem on the union debate when a parliamentary resolution was adopted on Tanganyikan government.

> The most recent example is the G55 (1993) resolution demanding a separate government for Tanganyika. Mwalimu wrote a poem (*shairi*) of over 200 verses whose thrust was simultaneously to argue that it was parliamentary resolution only in name; that the secret pilots were the existing top leadership of the party. The driving force (*msukumo*) was tribalism (*ukabila*) and religious bigotry (*udini*) and that the whole argument of parliamentary resolution as a demand of the people was a thin masquerade for the presidential ambitions of the then two top leaders. This very driving force he warned, would not only disintegrate the Union but Tanganyika itself (Shivji 2007, p. 59).

From the poem it is evident that Mwalimu had been consistently advocating equality and national unity and was against the leaders who wanted to use the opportunity for their own political ends.

Nyerere's artistic skills date back to when he was young and wrote an essay to express his ideas on the issues that affect the daily lives of women. At the age of 22, Nyerere had already read and was influenced by the works of scholars such as John Stuart Mill. According to an interview with Ikaweba Bunting, Nyerere explains:

> I wrote an essay in 1944 called 'The Freedom of Women'. I must be honest and say I was influenced by John Stuart Mill, who had written about the subjugation of women. My father had 22 wives and I knew how hard they had to work and what they went through as women. Here in this essay I was moving towards the idea of freedom theoretically. But I was still in the mindset of improving the lives and welfare of Africans: I went to Tabora to start teaching.
>
> (Bunting 2007, p. 66)

The Tanzanian coat of arms, a national symbol, represents the artistic creativity contained in other symbols such as the flag, the national anthem and the uhuru torch. It is moulded to embrace the warrior's shield in the midst of elephant tusks mounted on top of Mount Kilimanjaro. One can also see the man on the left and the woman on the right, standing in balanced postures on the sides of the warrior's shield with cloves and cotton on their feet respectively. The warrior's shield has the uhuru torch, Tanzanian flag, crossed axe and hoe, spear and water sign. All these symbolise the motto below: *Uhuru na Umoja* (Freedom and Unity) – the title of Nyerere's (1966) book. It is important to notice that the warrior's shield depicts various historical battles for freedom. The man and woman reflect respect for human equality regardless of gender, colour or any other social element.

As pointed out earlier, the establishment of the Ministry of Culture was the earliest post-independence initiative to fight against cultural imperialism. According to Ngugi:

> Cultural imperialism in the era of neocolonialism can be a dangerous cancer because it can take new, subtle forms. It can hide under cloaks of militant nationalism, calls for dead authenticity, performances of cultural symbolism, and even under native racist self-assertive banners that are often a substitute for national self-criticism and collective pride in the culture and history of resistance.
>
> (Ngugi 1997, p. 18)

As Ngugi explained, Nyerere evidently knew the consequences and magnitude of cultural imperialism and he took measures to overcome it. He believed that a people's language was an important factor in this struggle. He devised subtle modalities to absorb imperialist influences in the theatre. The immediate approach was to provide artists with the theme of their performances – Ujamaa. Since artists looked at Nyerere as a national and international role model, they could easily transform his actions and decisions into theatrical works. The philosophical speeches and arguments which Nyerere preferred to deliver were probably among those which influenced artists.

The other theatrical landmark was the birth of Chama cha Mapinduzi (CCM) in 1977. This political party was the result of the merger of TANU and the Afro-Shirazi Party (ASP). After the birth of CCM, Hiari ya Moyo composed a song titled *Leo Sio Sherehe Tunaanza Chama* (Today is not a ceremony, we are inaugurating a party).

Kufa kwa TANU na Afro	The death of TANU and Afro [ASP]
Sio kufikiwa kwa Ujamaa kamili	Is not the attainment of Ujamaa
Wametimiza yao waliyoyaweza	They have fulfilled what they could
CCM lake ni kuendeleza	CCM has the responsibility to take over
Kwenye Ujamaa kutufikisha	So as to reach Ujamaa

(Semzaba 1983, p. 26)

This was the time when we were told *chama kimeshika hatamu* (party supremacy) had to come first. Therefore even artistic works, especially songs and performances, by the NAGs, were geared towards party supremacy and the promotion of Ujamaa. Mlama (1991, p. 103) adds, 'the ideological intention behind the promotion of these groups [NAGs] resulted in the development of a theatre for propaganda which ... is an attempt to domesticate the theatre to serve the interest of the ruling ideology'.

Despite all these efforts by Nyerere, there was no defined socialist cultural policy (Mlama 1985). The 1962 and subsequent speeches were taken as part of the art/cultural policy. The so-called policy was based on the state officials' statements. It thus was taken for granted that the growth of culture would go hand in hand with the success of Ujamaa:

This argument ignores the fact that the economic base and the cultural superstructure determine and influence each other and cannot therefore be separated. It also ignores the fact that while the country is waiting for socialist culture to come it is under constant exposure to the influences of capitalist and imperialist culture which is part and parcel of the imperialist struggle against socialism. There is a tendency to think that the war against imperialism is only an economic one, and a failure to realise that imperialism is fighting the war against socialism both economically and culturally.

(Mlama 1985, p. 5)

Unfortunately, the ministry or department which was designed for arts and culture has been shunted around several places since 1962. By 1995, the ministry, or its culture component, had been shifted into about 11 ministries and offices (Askew 2002, p. 186). This frequent change has been taken to mean a lack of seriousness about matters to do with culture, especially the arts (Askew 2002, Lange 2002, Lihamba 1985b, Mlama 1985). Instead of working on a clear cultural policy that could comply with Ujamaa, the ministry responsible for culture was busy sending groups to perform at party-state meetings and functions. This was partly due to the influence of Ujamaa ideology and party supremacy as during that time all directives from the state/party top leaders were geared towards cultivating the ruling party and its ideology. Giving several examples, Mlama confirmed that 'this tendency has given rise to puppet art which largely parrots what the leaders are saying' (Mlama 1985, p. 14).

To protect the supremacy of the party, Radio Tanzania-Dar es Salaam (RTD) and the National Music Council (BAMUTA) ended up exercising direct censorship, which was carried out by cultural officers at all levels (Mlama 1985, pp. 14–15). Mlama (1985, p. 15) noted that 'such control betrays a misguided view of the role of art in ideology. Art can be critical and yet contribute positively to ideological development. Parrot art does not contribute to the socialist construction because it does not analyse problems and point out solutions.'

Although Mwalimu was an artist, fond of art and a good teacher, he was not lucky enough to persuade his fellow politicians, especially in his party, to appreciate making art out of political propaganda. Nyerere's speeches were misinterpreted to mean sending a group of *ngoma* dancers to the airport or to the national stadium to dance in the harsh sun and show themselves to the guests of 'honour' while security officers were busy strangling their movements and tempering their emotions even before they started to perform. This was happening at the same time that Nyerere's ideas were being implemented with political slogans like *kazi si lele mama* (work is not a dance of *lele mama*) which directly abuse arts (Mlama 1985 p.17).

Mwalimu's love for art was not spared by imperialism either. The proposal to restructure the economy through the International

Monetary Fund (IMF) and World Bank's structural adjustment pro-grammes (SAPs) necessitated the downsizing of state expenditure. In addition to the NAGs' other artistic and political challenges, by the end of the 1970s the government could no longer subsidise them. The government's focus was on repaying debts through the withdrawal of budget allocations to social services such as theatre and 'ploughing' towards development, modernity and universal-ism, in other words complying with neoliberal policies.

It is therefore important to emphasise that the project to build national culture through theatre was dismantled when the state had to downsize its expenditure in order to comply with the IMF and World Bank neoliberal conditions. 'Throughout the country, government-owned institutions were either scrapped, had to curtail their activities or were later privatised. Cultural troupes owned by such organisations ceased to function' (Lihamba 2004, p. 243). At the end, 'liberalisation policies pursued from the early 1980s made theatre a commodity for sale like any other' (Rubin and Diakante 2001, p. 304).

The state dissolved the NAGs and instead, formed a national art institute in 1980. This institute was situated in Ilala Sharif-Shamba in Dar es Salaam, in the current National Art Council (BASATA) premises. In 1981, the institute was transformed and shifted to Bagamoyo and became Bagamoyo College of Arts (BCA); currently it is known as the Institute of Arts and Culture, Bagamoyo or TaSUBa (Makoye 1998, p. 95).

To ensure sustainability of the arts, Nyerere created oppor-tunities for artists to produce and survive on their own. Despite the fact that there was no clear policy, his speeches were mostly translated as policy directives. From his speeches one could sense his ideas, creativity and passion for art. He established Nyumba ya Sanaa (a house for artists) in 1974, positioning it in the middle of Dar es Salaam. He believed that if it could be efficiently utilised, it would reduce the syndrome of artists needing to beg to donors and the state, which enslaves them. It is surprising to note that even Nyumba ya Sanaa has been one of the places the state wants to privatise while at the same time struggling to secure funds to build other places of the same nature in Bagamoyo (Naluyaga 2009).

The Zanzibar Declaration of 1991, which replaced the Arusha

Declaration (1967), could be regarded as the 'marketisation of arts' like any other product (Rubin and Diakante 2001). Artists, who are supposed to compete in this market, were not well equipped to cope with the changes in terms of competition and producing quality works. Art education could be one way in which the state assists them. The 1997 Cultural Policy's (*Sera ya Utamaduni*) clauses 2.1.2 (p. 4) and 6.2.5 (p. 19) stated the necessity of introducing arts (music, fine art, sculpture and the performing arts) as examinable subjects in both primary and secondary schools (Wizara ya Elimu na Utamaduni 1997). It was not until 2008 that the government implemented such provisions.

Although the outcomes of the 1997 Cultural Policy are yet to be realised, a number of challenges can be identified. Students are being oriented in the English language, which prevents them from understanding arts as a simulacrum of their culture which is mainly reflected in the Kiswahili language. Insufficient teachers, teaching and learning materials are some of the other challenges (Mmasy 2009). One might ask what the responsible ministry was preparing for.

While artistic works, as in any other sector, are expected to be market driven, piracy has remained a major setback for the artists and the national economy. Perhaps if Tanzania strengthened its tax collection and protection of artistic works, they could have contributed to the national economy. In Nigeria, the video industry is the third contributor to GDP preceded only by the oil and telecommunications industries (Palmberg 2008). This implies that if Mwalimu's ideas could have been properly implemented, there would be no need for artists to wait on the mercy of donors or depend on the state. Instead, artists could be supporting themselves and the collected taxes could be contributing to other developmental projects. This illustrates that Mwalimu's ideas could have coped with the challenges brought about by market-driven forces.

References

Askew, K.M. (2002) *Performing the Nation: Swahili Music and Cultural Politics in Tanzania*, Chicago, University of Chicago Press

Bakari, J.A. and Materego, G.R. (2008) *Sanaa kwa Maendeleo: Stadi, Mbinu na Mazoezi*, Moshi, Viva Productions

Bunting, I. (2007) 'The heart of Africa: interview with Julius Nyerere on anti-colonialism', in H. Othman (ed) *Sites of Memory: Julius Nyerere and the Liberation Struggle of Southern Africa*, Zanzibar, ZIFF, pp. 64–9

Chachage, C.S. (1986) 'Socialist ideology and the reality of Tanzania', PhD thesis, University of Glasgow

Chachage, C.S. (2002) *Utandawazi na Migogoro ya Utamaduni*, Dar es Salaam, University of Dar es Salaam

Edmondson, L. (2007) *Performance and Politics in Tanzania: The Nation on Stage*, Bloomington, Indiana University Press

Erick, I. (2009) 'Ujamaa, Shetani na Mawingu: Aina za Vinyago Walivyochonga Wamakonde kwa Ubunifu', *Daily News*, http://www.habarileo.co.tz/biasharaFedha/index.php?id=4282, accessed 9 September 2009

Kerr, D. (1995) *African Popular Theatre: From Pre-Colonial Times to the Present Day*, London, James Currey

Lange, S. (1995) *From Nation-Building to Popular Culture: Modinisation of Performance in Tanzania*, Bergen, Charles Michelsen Institute

Lange, S. (2002) 'Managing modernity: gender, state, and nation in the popular drama of Dar es Salaam', PhD thesis, University of Bergen

Lihamba, A. (1985a) 'Politics and theatre after the Arusha Declaration, 1967–1984', PhD thesis, University of Leeds

Lihamba, A. (1985b) 'The performing arts and development', *Utafiti*, vol. 7, no. 1, pp. 30–9

Lihamba, A. (2004) 'Tanzania', in M. Banham (ed) *A History of Theatre in Africa*, Cambridge, Cambridge University Press, pp. 233–46

Makoye, H.F. (1998) 'Dance research in Tanzania', *Dance Research Journal*, vol. 30, no.1, pp. 95–7

Mazrui, A.A. and Mazrui, A.M. (1995) *Swahili State and Society: The Political Economy of an African Language*, Nairobi, East African Educational Publishers

Mlama, P.O. (1985) 'Tanzania's cultural policy and its implications for the contribution of the arts to socialist development', *Utafiti*, vol. 7, no. 1, pp. 9–19

Mlama, P.O. (1991) *Culture and Development: The Popular Theatre Approach to Africa*, Uppsala, Scandnavian Institute of African Studies

Mmasy, G. (2009) 'Setbacks on implementing new theatre art syllabus', http://thebrightshadow.blogspot.com/, accessed 16 September 2009

Mollel, T.M. (1985) 'African theatre and the colonial legacy: review of the East African scene', *Utafiti*, vol. 7, no. 1, pp. 20–9

Mwangi, E. (2009) 'Amandina Lihamba's gendered adaptation of Sembene Ousmane's The Money-Order', *Research in African Literatures*, vol. 40, no. 3 pp. 149–73

Naluyaga, R. (2009) 'Nyumba ya Sanaa in a mess', http://www.afrum.com/index.php?hash=9ac1766a68261c041609495b1a423be6&categ=art_cur&action=vypis&select=394, accessed 9 July 2009

Ngugi wa Thiong'o (1997) *Writers in Politics: A Re-engagement with Issues of Literature and Society*, Oxford, James Currey

Nsekela, A.J. (1984) *Time to Act*, Dar es Salaam, Dar es Salaam University Press

Nyerere, J. (1966) *Freedom and Unity/Uhuru na Umoja*, Dar es Salaam, Oxford University Press

Othman, H. (2007) Mwalimu Julius Nyerere: An Intellectual in Power, in H. Othman (ed) *Sites of Memory: Julius Nyerere and the Liberation Struggle of Southern Africa*, Zanzibar, ZIFF, pp. 70–81

Palmberg, M. (2008) 'Nollywood – a new African popular culture', in *Africa on the Global Agenda*, Uppsala, Nordiska Afrikainstitutet, pp. 37–40

Plastow, J. (1996) *African Theatre and Politics, The Evolution of Theatre in Ethiopia, Tanzania and Zimbabwe. A Comparative Study*, Amsterdam, Rodopi

Ranger, T. (1975) *Dance and Society in Eastern Africa 1890–1970*, Nairobi, Heinemann Educational Books

Rubin, D. and Diakante, O.N. (eds) (2001) *The World Encyclopaedia of Contemporary Theatre: Africa*, London, Routledge

Semzaba, E. (1983) 'Trends in modern theatre movement', MA thesis, University of Dar es Salaam

Shivji, I. (2007) 'The mwalimu in Nyerere', in H. Othman (ed) *Sites of Memory: Julius Nyerere and the Liberation Struggle of Southern Africa*, Zanzibar, ZIFF, pp. 58–63

Wizara ya Elimu na Utamaduni (1997) *Sera ya Utamaduni*, Dar es Salaam.

Mwalimu and the state of education

Chambi Chachage

'Yet Primary Education for all, at least in Africa, requires full commitment from the State'

Mwalimu Julius Kambarage Nyerere on education and development in Africa

Introduction

If there is one theme that was very dear to Julius K. Nyerere it is education. He thought about it, he spoke about it, he even wrote about it. No wonder he is called Mwalimu, 'The Teacher'.

A two-volume collection entitled *Nyerere on Education* published in 2004 and 2006 respectively reveals that about 35 essays and speeches on the theme are attributed to his name. This chapter is a critical review of the thoughts and practices of Mwalimu on this theme of *elimu* in relation to the current state of education in Tanzania. It is thematically divided into three main sections, which are entitled after Nyerere's speeches on 'The power of teachers', 'A great urge for education' and 'Education for service and not for selfishness', which he delivered in 1966, 1954 and 1999 respectively.

The power of teachers

Julius K. Nyerere was a teacher by profession. He earned a diploma in education in 1945 at what was then Makerere University College in Uganda. Probably, like many teachers today, his choice of this career was an afterthought as the following biographical note by George Shepperson reveals:

> He admitted later, however, that while his first ambition was to be a government clerk, he then became interested in medicine and made the final decision to become a teacher at the last minute, making up his mind only when he was filling in his application form for college.
>
> (Molony 2000, p. 7)

The teachers of our times would surely relate to his experience of declining 'the offer to teach at Tabora Government School' upon his graduation and choosing instead 'to teach Biology and History at St Mary's, a new Catholic secondary school in Tabora' (Molony 2000, p. 7). By the time he left to pursue further studies at Edinburgh University in Scotland, Mwalimu was politically conscious. However, as William E. Smith (1973) and John C. Hatch (1976) document, he is on record as claiming that his self-evolved ideas on politics were formed completely at Edinburgh, where his strongest subject was philosophy.

While at Edinburgh he became better acquainted with the philosophical works associated with social democratic liberalism. Of particular interest to him were the treatises of the father of Utilitarianism and a philosopher of education, John Stuart Mill, whom he admired a lot. However, he was to admit later after Uhuru: 'I was concerned about education; the work of Booker T. Washington resonated with me' (Nyerere quoted in Bunting 1999).

When he came back to Tanganyika in 1952 he joined St Francis' College in Pugu as a teacher of history. Tanazanian educators who have recently been debating an attempt to stop them being involved in politics would relate to Mwalimu's experience of having to quit shortly thereafter what was a relatively lucrative job. He had to resign from the teaching post so as to be a politician.

Having personally experienced the perils and pleasures of teaching, Mwalimu was always concerned about the plights and prospects of teachers. In his review of Nyerere's 1966 remarks at Morogoro Teachers College, Jenerali Ulimwengu (2004) notes how Mwalimu 'is at pains to dispel the popular perception of teachers as a powerless group'. Sadly, this perception persists today. Mwalimu was correct in calling it 'one of the biggest fallacies of our society. For teachers can make or ruin our society. As a group they have power which is second to none. It is not the power of a man with a gun; it is not a power which can be seen by a fool' (Nyerere 1968a, p. 228).

The teachers' threats to strike and the open strikes that hit Tanzania in late 2008 give a glimpse of this power. But there are also 'silent strikes' that go on each and every day. These involve deliberate absenteeism, lack of teaching motivation, being overwhelmed with the workload and so forth. The following confession captures the conditions that lead to these 'latent strikes':

> I am teaching Kiswahili and Mathematics and I have 16 periods per week. I do not have other responsibilities in school. In the classes that I teach there are between 120 and 150 pupils. This is a very unsatisfactory situation. Some pupils, especially those sitting at the back do not listen to you and as a result do not learn anything. Marking so many pupils' exercises books is another problem. I spend more time on marking than in teaching.
>
> (A female grade A teacher in Ludewa Urban, quoted in HakiElimu 2004, p. 19)

It is not surprising then that some teachers interviewed in HakiElimu's (2004) study on *The Living and Working Conditions of Teachers in Tanzania* were nostalgic about the times of Mwalimu. To them those were the days when teachers 'were respected a lot' and the 'salary you got was enough to live a decent life'. Of course some things have improved since the multidimensional crisis that faced the education sector during the structural adjustment programmes (SAPs) that were introduced in the 1980s. As Rakesh Rajani (2003) optimistically observed in the wake of the Primary Education Development Plan (PEDP), the announcement of the PEDP brought about real hope and change, which included the recruitment of about 7,000 teachers.

The PEDP aimed to 'recruit adequate number of new teachers'; 'establish a teacher-to-pupil ratio that effectively accommodates enrolment increases'; 'ensure equitable and gender-balanced distribution of trained teachers'; and 'improve the use of existing teachers.' To that end the plan made 'provisions for teacher training and upgrading' as well as 'strengthening the skills of existing teachers' (Rajani 2003, p. 5). But not everything went according to plan. For instance, HakiElimu's (2005) *Three Years of PEDP Implementation: Key Findings from Government Reviews* revealed that 1,064 more than the targeted numbers of teachers were recruited. However, this report also revealed that the teacher-to-pupil ratio had increased from 1:46 to 1:59, indicating that the PEDP targets for teacher recruitment were an underestimate. The consolidated review also revealed that the distribution of trained teachers within regions and districts remained problematic as teachers were unwilling to be posted to remote areas. HakiElimu's (2007) update, *What has been Achieved in Primary Education? Key Findings from Government Reviews*, found that recruitment does not necessarily translate into teachers in classrooms since of the 10,510 pupil teachers who were deployed to schools in 2006 only 7,271 reported on duty.

The situation by the end of 2009 had not improved significantly. For instance, on the basis of official sources such as the latest *Basic Education Statistics in Tanzania (BEST)* (URT 2009) and *Poverty and Human Development Reports (PHDR)* (URT 2007), HakiElimu and IDASA (2009) noted that the teacher-to-pupil ratio deteriorated as it moved from 1:53 in 2002 to 1:57during the first year of the PEDP. By the year the PEDP ended, however, the rate had improved slightly to 1:52. This, the joint study revealed, could partly be attributed to the massive campaign of fast tracking the training of school leavers and recruiting them as teachers.

These teachers are sometimes referred to pejoratively as 'Yebo Yebo' or 'Vodafasta' – a quick Vodacom network commercial product – to stress their lack of prior qualifications, proper training and the requisite skills. Such derogatory perceptions and the degraded training plans are the hallmark of what Mwalimu referred to as one of the biggest fallacies of our society. As the study further noted, in 2007 the ratio deteriorated again to its 2002 figure, i.e. 1:53, prompting the PHDR2007 to realistically admit that 'it is unlikely that the National Strategy for Growth and Reduction of Poverty's (MKUKUTA) target of 1:45 by 2010 will be reached' (URT 2007, p. 27). Predictably, according to the BEST statistics (URT 2009), the ratio is 1:54 for both 2008 and 2009, a far cry from the 2010 target.

The primary leavers examination results (PSLE) for 2009 also give us a glimpse of the state of education. More than 50 per cent of the students who sat the exam failed. The minister responsible for education was quoted by the media as attributing this poor performance to mass failures in mathematics and English: 20.96 per cent of the students passed the former whilst over 35.44 per cent passed the latter. Tellingly, the minister said: 'We are trying to address these problems by training teachers in the two subjects and also improving the curriculum so that we can get more competent teachers for the two subjects' (*The Citizen* 2009a, p. 17).

It is quite clear that we did not really listen when 'Mwalimu decries the fact that teachers are usually underestimated and accorded less social recognition than they deserve' (Ulimwengu 2004, p. 4). We haven't really made sense of what he means when he 'points to the tendency to ignore teachers and explains that this is so because teachers, unlike civil servants, do not wield obvious power' (Ulimwengu 2004, p. 4). If we really understood him then we wouldn't have a situation such as the one documented by HakiElimu and IDASA (2009): when Ludewa's district education officer in Iringa region was asked why Masimavalafu primary school tended to come last in the PSLE, he responded that it was because for a long time it had only one teacher. We would not have a situation whereby parents in many areas of our country have to volunteer to hire temporary teachers because those deployed by the government do not report to work or opt for other career opportunities as 'their living standards are at low levels and many are not attracted to become teachers' (HakiElimu 2004, p. 13). By ignoring teachers we are embracing that biggest fallacy of our society even though 'the truth is that it is teachers, more than any other single group of people ... who shape the ideas and aspirations of the nation' (Nyerere 1968a, p. 226).

A great urge for education

As a teacher and parent Mwalimu had a great awareness of the need for education since colonial times. It is not surprising, then, that Julius K. Nyerere's (2004a) first speech to the colonial Legislative Council in 1954 is now documented under the title 'A great urge for education'. He referred to it as a 'healthy urge' and used it to argue against the colonial government's quest to cut down expenditure that would affect this basic service. Looking to the future, way beyond the colonial period, he questioned the rate and target of primary school expansion thus:

It is a great success, but is it enough? By 1956 we shall still have 64 percent of our children of primary school age outside the schools. We have been reducing our illiteracy by about 2 percent per year. After 1956, if we continue at that rate of reducing our illiteracy of that age group at 2 percent a year it will take us another thirty or more years, after 1956, before we have all our children of primary school age at school. That is somewhere about 1986 or 1990. I do not think, sir, that this gives us any cause for complacency in the matter of education, and it must be remembered, sir, that this target we are aiming at is a target for children of primary school age in this country, and in other countries also, form about one-third of all the children of school-going age. So that even after 1956, when we have attained a target of 36 percent it is not really 36 percent of all our children, and I feel sir, that in this matter we cannot talk of cutting down expenditure in education, because the country needs education, it needs it very badly. I think our duty is to supply, to try to supply this demand.

(Nyerere 2004a, p. 3)

Here Mwalimu is talking in easy-to-understand language about what our education experts refer to – by way of contrast – as the 'gross enrolment ratio' (GER) and 'net enrolment ratio' (NER). He is arguing that the government should not only be concerned about the former, which is defined as the number 'of pupils in the official age group for a given level of education enrolled in that level expressed as a percentage of the total population in that age group' (URT 2009, p. xv). It should also be concerned about the latter case, which includes the number 'of pupils enrolled in a given level of education, regardless of age, expressed as percentage of the population in relevant official age group' (URT 2009, p. xv). No wonder when he became the first president of an independent Tanganyika and, subsequently, a united republic of Tanzania he worked hard to ensure that all people, young and old, had access to basic education and 'mastering' the 'the three Rs'.

In the case of the young ones his government came up with a nationwide campaign for universal primary education (UPE) as a response to popular demands, and in the case of the old ones it carried out a massive campaign on adult education. Abolition of school fees towards the end of the 1960s and the beginning of the 1970s, as Marjorie Mbilinyi (2003) notes, was a first and necessary step towards UPE. However, as she further notes, UPE was truly achieved with the implementation of the Musoma Resolution of 1974, which called for a UPE national campaign. In a nostalgic tone she concludes:

> Contrary to revisionist views today, UPE was highly successful; at least in quantitative terms. By 1984, the number of children in school had doubled: more than 90% of school-aged children were enrolled in school, a higher proportion than found in most other African countries, including those in the middle and high income groups. Of even greater significance to women, UPE led to gender parity in primary school enrolment. The proportion of boys and girls in primary school became equal as a result of UPE.
>
> (Mbilinyi 2003, p. 2)

As far as adult education is concerned Tanzania made provision to start an institute to cater for it. The government also instituted a legal and policy framework for adult learning. 'When this proviso was implemented with some seriousness,' Salma Maoulidi (2004) notes, 'Tanzania achieved one of the highest literacy levels, not only in the continent, but also in the world.' She was referring to the 1970s when Mwalimu Nyerere made it his personal as well as the national mission to ensure that as many adults as possible were able to read and write. By the time he passed on the baton of the country's presidency, as Maoulidi (2008) notes elsewhere, illiteracy for the population aged 13 years and above was systematically reduced to 10 per cent.

Today the great urge for education is still there. It is not that easy to tell whether it is still a healthy urge as we are no longer very sure about the kind of education we need. The fact that the language of instruction in public primary schools is different to that in secondary schools has created a system that produces graduates that are not sufficiently literate in English or as one of the leading critics of the use of English as the language of instruction puts it: 'The use of a medium of instruction that the majority of students do not understand denies students the chance to be active learners and remain passive observers absorbing all that is said without asking questions' (Martha Qorro 2001, p. 114). In fact this language policy has caused a number of parents and students to conflate 'knowledge' or 'education' with 'English' and as a result they opt to send their children to private 'English-medium academies' for primary education. It has also fuelled support for the use of English, the so-called language of globalisation, rather than Kiswahili as the medium of instruction in public primary schools. The following email response to my article on 'What about a stimulus package for the education crisis?' (*The Citizen* 2009b) from a university student, reproduced here without any changes, gives a glimpse of the urgency of the situation:

> Man i read ur article on THE CITIZEN today honesty u did a good job, but i can tell u one thing we cant just talk to help our young brothers n sisters to pass english subject without knowing that those primary teachers are those who fail in O-LEVEL EDUCATION, what is needed is improving the availability of good english teachers in our schools, til when the government will stop gives us the wrong teachers, when i was in primary shool standard 5 to, i thanks god that ma daddy new that those teachers are fake, then he find a teacher from st.maries and that teacher was paid to teach me only english language and i thanks god coz its governing me up to now, i dont even remember ma school english teacher but i remember that one from st. maries its fun, i was asking one of ma friend at school if she has the extra pen to borrow me n she said 'I DONT KNOW ' she was believing that she means 'i dont have' its very funny but i knew that she dont know what she was talking about n we was at std 7 at dat time can u just imagine. so this is the crisis, thanks man 4 ur article makes me remember far away n i can c now u also c it 2.

Education for service and not for selfishness

Mwalimu Nyerere's 1999 call for 'Education for service and not for selfishness' was an attempt to couch his 1967 policy of education for self-reliance and 1974's motto of 'Education for liberation' in the parlance of today (Nyerere 1968b). As The Open University of Tanzania (1999) reminds us, they were his last words on education. We therefore have to pay particular attention to this speech as it sums up his overall stance on this theme.

He starts by using the Maxim gun as an analogy for education, poetically reminding us that it will be used by those who have it against those who do not. 'The instrument of domination of the future', he aptly predicts, 'is going to be education.' He then optimistically assures us that fortunately 'in the acquisition of that instrument we can all compete and all win with honour' (Nyerere 1999, p. 3). Unfortunately, as the statistics cited above indicate, this is not what we are doing. Instead we have created a system that ensures that there is no 'place for everyone at the rendezvous of victory' to use a phrase that was popularised by his contemporary, Aimé Césaire. A seasoned educator had this to say about such a system:

> Tanzania has a deeply unequal, dualistic education system, one for the rich, and one for the poor, with an education system of 'best' public schools for the middle classes. This stands in stark contrast to the principles of equity and justice promoted by Mwalimu. The marker of difference is no longer race as it was in the colonial days, but class. We may find, shortly, that class inequalities are far more divisive, bearing within them profound implications for social cohesion in the country.
>
> (Marjorie Mbilinyi 2004, p. xvi)

It is in this class sense that Nyerere urges us to enter what he refers to as 'this honourable competition for knowledge' if 'we do not want to be the permanent source of the hewers of wood and drawers of water for the educated of this world' (Nyerere 1999, p. 4). To do so, he reiterates his lifelong position: our primary school education should be universal. Gender conscious as he was when he penned his essay on 'The freedom of women' in 1944 at Makerere, Mwalimu Nyerere warns us that if this education is not universal 'those who will miss out will be mostly girls'. In the light of this caution it is worth commending the government for allowing pregnant girls to continue with their studies after giving birth. In this honourable competition, as Mwalimu admonishes us, our education should be of good quality. His insistence on this is powerful and still very relevant today; it deserves to be quoted in full:

> Primary education in particular should be excellent; for this is the only formal education that most Tanzanians are likely to receive. At present the quality of our primary school education is appalling. We must do something about it, as a matter of National urgency. Apart from the fact that it is the education of the vast majority of the citizens of Tanzania, it is also the foundation of

183

the whole of our Education System. *Ndiyo Elimu ya Msingi*. If it is poor the rest of our Education System is bound to suffer.

(Nyerere 1999, p. 4)

It is an indisputable fact that our secondary and tertiary education is suffering because of this appalling *msingi* (foundation). Further statistics that prove this are those on the percentage of students passing the form 4 examinations. As HakiElimu and IDASA (2009) observed, BEST 2009 indicates that even the 'only slight improvement from 33.6% in 2006 to 35.7% in 2007' (URT 2007, p. 30) presented in PHDR 2007 did not occur after all. Rather, the rate stagnated at 35.6 per cent for both years and it deteriorated further to 26.7 per cent in 2008. This indicator only includes students who get divisions 1 to 3. Ironically, overall, most students get division 4, which is still not considered to be a failure by the ministry responsible for education. In fact it was also observed that since 2000 over 50 per cent of students have been getting this division, the peak being 56.9 per cent in 2008. The results for 2009 were not out as I and the authors of the HakiElimu and IDASA (2009) report were writing.

Mwalimu also notes that our education should be relevant to our needs. We cannot compete if the majority of our people and their descendants live in villages and yet 'we refuse to give those children an education that could help them to improve their own lives in the villages' (Nyerere 1999, p. 6). It is in this regard that Mwalimu Nyerere advocated a policy of education for self-reliance, which aimed at providing a complete education by the time students completed their primary education. It is also in this regard that he conceptualised education for liberation:

I emphasise this point because of my profound belief in the power of education. For a poor people like us Education should be an instrument of liberation; it should never be so irrelevant or otherworldly as to become an instrument of alienation. Alienation from yourself, because it makes you despise yourself; an alienation from the community in which you live because it purports to make you different without making you useful to anybody, including yourself.

(Nyerere 1999, p. 6)

It is thus a saddening fact that a significant number of our students complete their primary, secondary or even tertiary education without the requisite skills for competing in the so-called global village. As HakiElimu's (2008) *What is Quality Education? A Research on Citizens' Perspectives and Children's Basic Skills* reveals, the overall competency levels in mathematics – a subject that is the basis of computation – was very low for both primary and secondary school students. It also revealed that their reading skills in English – the so-called 'Kiswahili of the world' – were poorly developed, especially in primary schools even though they were – and are still – required to be taught in English when they enter secondary schools. Indeed, this area of language policy is one that Mwalimu is said to have regretted not having changed. It is about time that we rectify this confused language policy if we are to ensure that knowledge is really transferred from the teachers to the students. That can be done through a language that both teachers and students are familiar with. In the case of Tanzania such a language is Kiswahili.

In his conclusion Mwalimu add another important ingredient that, in relative terms, we lack today:

Finally, our education, especially our higher education, should be socially responsible. Education for Self-Reliance is not Education for Selfishness. Yes, it is for Self-Reliance of the individual, but it is also for the Self-Reliance of our country. I believe that the community has a responsibility to educate its members. The need for individuals to contribute directly to their own education and the education of their children cannot absolve the community as a whole, represented by local and central government, from its duty to assist every Tanzanian to receive a good education. But a poor country like Tanzania cannot afford to educate the selfish. It invests in education in the belief that such investment is good for both the individual concerned and for the community as a whole. In the language of yesterday: Education for Self-Reliance, especially at this higher level, should also be Education for Service. Not all of us will have the same concept of community, but all of us have a need to belong. However socially insensitive we may be, we have a need to belong to a community of fellow human beings. No human can make it alone. Nobody is asking us to love others more than we love ourselves; but those of us who have been lucky enough to receive a good education have a duty also to help to improve the well-being of the community to which we belong: it is part of loving ourselves!

(Nyerere 1999, p. 9-10)

Conclusion

Mwalimu Nyerere's legacy is tied to the history of the education sector in Tanzania. His regime produced positive as well as negative results in education. Universal primary education stands out as a positive, while the confused language of instruction policy stands out for me as a negative. Here I agree with the assessment that 'Nyerere's own views were also contradictory, in that he endorsed both developmentalist and emancipatory ones' whereby the 'former prioritised experts, rather than mobilisation of the people to organise on their own behalf' (Mbilinyi 2004, p. xiii).

However, I do not endorse the assessment that his policy on education was the total failure that neoliberal revisionists, nay, ahistorical critics, present to counter our nationalist history as they attempt to erase what we achieved from our consciousness. No one is better posed to respond to their historical amnesia than Mwalimu himself. I doubt he had a better response than this:

> At the World Bank the first question they asked me was 'how did you fail?' I responded that we took over a country with 85 per cent of its adult population illiterate. The British ruled us for 43 years. When they left, there were 2 trained engineers and 12 doctors. This is the country we inherited. When I stepped down there was 91-per-cent literacy and nearly every child was in school. We trained thousands of engineers and doctors and teachers. In 1988 Tanzania's per-capita income was $280. Now, in 1998, it is $140. So I asked the World Bank people what went wrong. Because for the last ten years Tanzania has been signing on the dotted line and doing everything the IMF and the World Bank wanted. Enrolment in school has plummeted to 63 per cent and conditions in health and other social services have deteriorated. I asked them again: 'what went wrong?' These people just sat there looking at me. Then they asked what could they do? I told them have some humility. Humility – they are so arrogant!
>
> (Nyerere in Bunting 1999)

Many parents can't afford schooling. A lot of students are not learning. Let's have some humility.

References

Bunting, Ikaweba (1999) 'The heart of Africa: interview with Julius Nyerere on anti-colonialism', *New Internationalist*, no. 309, January–February, http://www.hartford-hwp.com/archives/30/049.html, accessed 21 December 2009

Citizen, The (2009a) 'Boys dominate again in standard 7 Exams', 11 December

Citizen, The (2009b) 'What about a stimulus package for the education crisis?', 15 December

HakiElimu (2004) *The Living and Working Conditions of Teachers in Tanzania: A Research Report*, Dar es Salaam, HakiElimu

HakiElimu (2005) *Three Years of PEDP Implementation: Key Findings from Government Reviews – July 2005*, Dar es Salaam, HakiElimu

HakiElimu (2007) *What has been Achieved in Primary Education? Key Findings from Government Reviews – October 2007*, Dar es Salaam, HakiElimu

HakiElimu (2008) *What is Quality Education? A Research Report on Citizen's Perspectives and Children's Basic Skills – May 2008*, Dar es Salaam, HakiElimu

HakiElimu and IDASA (2009 forthcoming) *Right to Know, Right to Information – A Baseline Study Report on Tanzania*, Dar es Salaam, HakiElimu

Hatch, John C. (1976) *Two African statesmen: Kaunda of Zambia and Nyerere of Tanzania*, London, UK, Secker and Warburg

Maoulidi, Salma (2004) *Adult Education and Democracy*, HakiElimu Working Paper 04.5

Maoulidi, Salma (2008) 'In search of a framework for sustainable development through adult learning and education', http://udadisi.blogspot.com/2008/09/in-search-of-framework-for-sustainable_20.html, accessed 21 December 2009

Mbilinyi, Marjorie (2003) *Equity, Justice and Transformation in Education: The Challenge of Mwalimu Julius Nyerere Today*, HakiElimu Working Paper Series no. 2003.5.

Mbilinyi, Marjorie (2004) 'Introduction', in Lema, E., Mbilinyi, M. and Rajani, R. (eds) *Nyerere on Education/Nyerere Kuhusu Elimu*, Dar es Salaam, HakiElimu, E & D Limited and Mwalimu Nyerere Foundation, pp. vi–xvi.

Molony, Thomas (2000) 'Nyerere, the early years: a perspective from G. A. Shepperson', in Molony, T. and King, K. (eds) *Nyerere: Students, Teachers, Humanist, Statesman*, University of Edinburgh's Centre of African Studies Occasional Papers no. 84, pp. 3–18

Nyerere, Julius K. (1968a) 'The power of teachers' (1966) in J.K. Nyerere, *Freedom and Socialism*, Dar es Salaam, Oxford University Press, pp. 223–30

Nyerere, Julius K. (1968b) 'Education for self-reliance' (1967) in J.K. Nyerere, *Freedom and Socialism*, Dar es Salaam, Oxford University Press, pp. 267–90

Nyerere, Julius K. (1999) 'Education for service and not for selfishness', originally published in The Open University of Tanzania (1999)

'Mwalimu Julius K. Nyerere: His Last Words on Education', pp. 1–10 and reproduced in The Mwalimu Nyerere Foundation (2000) *Africa Today and Tomorrow*, pp. 70–4

Nyerere, Julius K. (2004a) 'A great urge for education' (1954) in Lema, E., Mbilinyi, M. and Rajani, R. (eds) *Nyerere on Education/Nyerere Kuhusu Elimu*, Dar es Salaam, HakiElimu, E & D Limited and Mwalimu Nyerere Foundation, pp. 1–5

Nyerere, Julius K. (2004b) 'Education for liberation' (1974) in Lema, E., Mbilinyi, M. and Rajani, R. (eds) *Nyerere on Education/Nyerere Kuhusu Elimu*, Dar es Salaam, HakiElimu, E & D Limited and Mwalimu Nyerere Foundation, pp. 121–32

Nyerere, Julius K. (2006) 'Education and development in Africa' (1996) in Lema, E., Omari, I. and Rajani, R. (eds) *Nyerere on Education/Nyerere Kuhusu Elimu*, vol. II, Dar es Salaam, HakiElimu, E & D Limited and Mwalimu Nyerere Foundation, pp. 206–12

Open University of Tanzania (1999) *Mwalimu Julius K. Nyerere: His Last Words on Education*, address by Mwalimu Julius K. Nyerere on the occasion of receiving an honorary doctorate of letters (*Honoris Causa*) from the Open University of Tanzania, 5 March

Qorro, Martha (2001) 'The language medium of instruction in Tanzanian secondary schools', in Lwaitama, A.F., Mtalo, E.G. and Mboma, L. (eds) *The Multi-Dimensional Crisis of Education in Tanzania: Debate and Action*, Dar es Salaam, University of Dar es Salaam Convocation, pp. 105–15

Rajani, Rakesh (2003) 'Is primary education heading in the right direction? Thinking with Nyerere', HakiElimu Working Paper Series no. 2003.4

Smith, William. E. (1973) *Nyerere of Tanzania*, London, Victor Gollancz

Ulimwengu, Jenerali (2004) 'Nyerere on education: a commentary', HakiElimu Working Paper 04.1

United Republic of Tanzania (URT) (2009) *Basic Education Statistics in Tanzania (BEST) 2005–2009: National Data*, July

United Republic of Tanzania (URT) (2007) *Poverty and Human Development Report (PHDR) 2007*

Index

SMS Uprising: Mobile Activism in Africa

Edited by Sokari Ekine

SMS Uprising brings together some of the best-known and experienced developers and users of mobile phone technologies in Africa to provide a unique insight into how activists and social change advocates are using them to facilitate change and address Africa's many challenges from within. These essays examine issues of inequality in access to mobile technologies and provide an overview of lessons learned without any of the romanticism so often associated with the use of new technologies for social change.

'This is a handbook for the small NGO or social change activist who is daunted by technology. Help is at hand, and *SMS Uprising* will help you find it.'

The Guardian

ISBN 978-1-906387-35-8   January 2010   152pp   £12.95

Food Rebellions! Crisis and the Hunger for Justice

Eric Holt-Giménez and Raj Patel

Food Rebellions! is a powerful handbook both examining our vulnerable food systems to reveal the root causes of the food crisis and proposing solutions. Democratising food systems can eliminate hunger and poverty. Farmers using sustainable approaches to production must be supported and their knowledge spread. In local, national and international policy arenas we need dialogue, transparency and a change to the 'rules' currently holding back agroecological alternatives.

'*Food Rebellions!* provides an analysis that is clear, documented and searing in its challenge ... I strongly endorse this book.'

Miguel d'Escoto Brockmann,
president of the 63rd General Assembly of the United Nations

ISBN 978-1-906387-30-3   July 2009   264pp   £16.95

 Order your copy from www.pambazukapress.org

Ending Aid Dependence

Yash Tandon

Developing countries can liberate themselves from the aid that pretends to be developmental but is not. This book shows how. It cautions against endorsing the collective colonialism of rich donor countries: an exit strategy from aid dependence requires a radical shift in both the mindset and the development strategy of countries dependent on aid.

'The message of this book needs to be seriously considered and debated by all those that are interested in the development of the countries of the South.'

Benjamin W. Mkapa, former President of Tanzania (1995-2005)

ISBN 978-1-906387-31-0   September 2008   144pp   £9.95

Where is Uhuru? Reflections on the Struggle for Democracy in Africa

Issa G. Shivji

Edited by Godwin Murunga

The neoliberal project, led by the IMF and World Bank, promised to correct many of the distortions in postcolonial Africa. Promises of liberalisation and democracy gave the project a level of legitimacy it otherwise would not have enjoyed. But neoliberalism failed to guarantee freedom, rights and prosperity. Issa G. Shivji shows how democratic politics, constitutionalism, land reform, women's rights and the Pan-Africanist project for emancipation have suffered, and proposes a new line of thinking embracing Africa's right to self-determination.

'*Where is Uhuru?* sharpens the content of the discussion and debate. It is recommended reading for those interested in the struggle for democracy and development in Africa.'

Salim Ahmed Salim, former secretary general of the Organization of African Unity (OAU)

ISBN 978-1-906387-46-4   April 2009   252pp   £16.95

 Order your copy from www.pambazukapress.org